Birthing God's Purpose

Birthing God's Purpose

How to Spiritually Fulfill God's
Command to Be Fruitful, Productive,
and Birth God's Purposes Upon Earth

by

DR. BILL HAMON

"Whatsoever is BORN of GOD overcomes"
1 John 5:4

BIRTHING GOD'S PURPOSE

Available through:
Dr. Bill Hamon
Christian International Ministries Network
P.O. Box 9000
Santa Rosa Beach, FL 32459 USA
(850) 231-4421

Distributed by:
Christian International Ministries Network
P.O. Box 9000
Santa Rosa Beach, FL 32459 USA
(850) 231-2600

ISBN 0-939868-08-3

Scripture quotations are taken from the New King James Version of the Bible unless otherwise noted.

TABLE OF CONTENTS

Resources Available from Christian International

Chapter 1

GOD WANTS YOU TO BIRTH HIS PURPOSE

"He who abides in Me, and I in him, bears much fruit." John 15:5

This book will give insight concerning fulfilling God's original command to His creation, mankind, to be fruitful and multiply. The divine principle of procreative productivity and multiplication is present in both the spirit realm and the natural realm. To fulfill our prophetic destiny, we must utilize the processes of divine productivity by understanding the principles of birthing God's purpose.

Adam and Eve were to be reproducers and reign over all God had created for them upon the earth. God said, "Be fruitful, multiply, reproduce, subdue and take dominion." (see Gen. 1:28) Adam and Eve were to reproduce humankind like unto themselves who were created in God's image and likeness. They were to perpetuate God's purpose and fulfill His plan for man and for all His natural creation on planet earth.

Mankind failed to reproduce people in God's image and likeness because of their sin of disobedience. Around 4,000 years later Jesus Christ came to earth to be born of a virgin woman in order to become a mortal human person. He became a mortal man so that He might redeem His fallen creation.   Jesus' death, burial, and resurrection became the gospel which, when believed and received, has the power to re-create man into a new creation in Christ Jesus.   Through Christ's cleansing blood and Holy Spirit mankind can be born again and become citizens of a new redeemed race called the Church.   This redeemed new creation race is destined to fulfill God's plan for humankind now in their mortal lives and to fulfill His original plan throughout eternity.

In this book we will cover how we spiritually fulfill God's command to be fruitful, productive, and birth God's purpose upon earth.   Jesus re-emphasized the command of Genesis 1:26-28 for His new creation in John 15:16, *"I chose you and appointed you that you should go and bear fruit and that your fruit should remain."*   Jesus declared that He is the true vine and His new creation are the branches and those who abide in Christ will bear much fruit.   *"And by this My Father is glorified, that you bear much fruit; so you will be my disciples."* (Jn. 15:8)

God promised the nation of Israel that if they would hear and obey His voice and keep His commandments that they would be fruitful in every area of their lives.   It is God's will that we be fruitful, productive, and have dominion in all areas of our lives.   However, the key is hearing and obeying God's voice and knowing how to cooperate with the Holy Spirit in allowing Him to impregnate us with a divine seed/revelation, and how to nurture and carry it in the womb of our spirit until God's time to birth it into His kingdom work.

A Message for All Christians

This message is very important and relevant for each and every one of us. It applies to all Christians - men and women, old and young.

It is the seed of God planted within us by the Holy Spirit that births the born again/new creation person in us. In all spiritual reality we are born of God, becoming children of God through the cleansing blood of God's only Son, Jesus Christ. It is also the Holy Spirit who makes us pregnant with the purposes of God, not whether we are male or female. I often tell men that they have to become comfortable with being the "Bride of Christ" and women must become comfortable being called "sons of God." In the same way, men must understand that they are called to conceive and birth God's purposes. When God began speaking these truths to me, I was not accustomed to thinking in these terms, yet God expanded my thinking to teach me His purposes.

Children are not too young to conceive something from God, nor is anyone too old in the natural. Samuel was a junior-age boy when God birthed His purpose in him, but Moses was 80 years old when he gave birth to God's purpose for his life. I conceived from God the revelation of the Prophetic Movement in 1983 at the age of 49, but it was not fully birthed until October 1988, five years later. We became "pregnant" with the Apostolic Movement in 1992 but it did not birth fully at Christian International until 1998. Then through prophetic/apostolic revelation, I became pregnant with the "Saints Movement" at age 62. I'm believing God for many more years of bearing fruit for Him.

Each one of us conceives something in our spirit which will eventually be born. Consider Psalm 7:14: *"He who is pregnant with evil and conceives trouble gives birth to disillusionment."* (NIV) If we don't want to conceive trouble, we must learn to align ourselves with God to birth His purposes!

A Message for Today

The whole creation is groaning in travail and laboring with birth pangs and with earnest expectation for the revealing of the sons of God, Christ's Church (Rom. 8:19, 22). The time is drawing near for the "Omega Generation," the last generation of the mortal Church, to come forth.

Since the primary purpose of this book is to help believers in the Lord Jesus Christ position themselves to be used of God to birth His purposes, it is written primarily for apostolic-prophetic Christians–those who have a "present truth" understanding of the moves of God. By "present truth" we are not implying that God's truth has ever changed, but rather that revelations and experiences which were revealed in the New Testament and actively practiced by the early Church, but lost during the Dark Ages, are progressively being restored to living, experiential reality in the Church. Since the time of the Protestant Reformation, the Holy Spirit has been bringing divine revelation and application of truths that were lost during the Middle Ages when the Church became increasingly bound by man-made tradition and legalism. For example, God worked through Martin Luther, John Calvin, and others to restore the truths of salvation by faith and the priesthood of all believers in what became known as the Protestant Movement.

Other major truths that have been restored to the Body of Christ include holiness; the present day operation of the gifts of the Holy Spirit including tongues, prophecy, healing, and miracles; and the restoration of apostles and prophets in the Church alongside pastors, evangelists, and teachers (the fivefold ministry - see Eph. 4:11). With godly Church government in order, the saints will be equipped to demonstrate the kingdom of God throughout the earth in what I have termed the "Saints Movement." This will bring the greatest harvest of souls the world has ever seen. Jesus will continue to build His Church until it becomes the fully mature Bride without spot or wrinkle for whom He is interceding and eagerly waiting.

God will birth all these things through His saints. If you are willing to subject your personal plans and goals to Christ's desire to build His Church, He will birth these things in and through you!

I am trusting that most of you will have knowledge and sufficient background in the areas that we will be covering, so I will not give a lot of historic background information here. If you would like more explanation of the restoration of Church truths, I encourage you to read my other books. *The Eternal Church* gives a description of each of the restoration movements and the truths they restored in detail. An in-depth treatment of the Prophetic and Apostolic Movements is given in *Prophets and the Prophetic Movement* and *Apostles, Prophets and the Coming Moves of God.*[1]

---

[1] Information for ordering resources is given in the back of this booklet.

Specific Relevance to Christian International

This message contains important truths which relate to the entire Body of Christ, but it also has more specific relevance and application to Christian International Ministries Network of which I am Bishop and apostolic overseer. The secondary purpose for which I have written this book is as a resource for ministers with the Christian International Network of Churches, Covenant Partners, and others whom God has called to co-labor with us in bringing forth His purposes.

We, at Christian International, know that we are just one small part of the hundreds of ministries and millions of individual members of the Body of Christ who are being used of God to fulfill His purpose. Mention of our own ministries is not for self promotion, but to use that which we know and have experienced to illustrate the Biblical principles of spiritual conception, pregnancy, and giving birth to something that Christ Jesus wants brought forth into His Church. Whether you are a part of CI or not, we trust that our story will encourage and bless you in your personal life and ministry.

Be Open to the Holy Spirit

I pray your heart will be open to what, I believe, the Holy Spirit wants to reveal. *"Lord, just open the hearts of those reading this right now to hear what You want to impart. Let Your Spirit bring revelation, application, understanding, anointing for receiving, and let there be a birthing within our spirits of that which You want us to be and do. In Jesus' Name, Amen."* (Eph. 1:18)

Chapter 2

KNOWING YOUR MEMBERSHIP MINISTRY AND PROPHETIC DESTINY

*"Now you are the body of Christ, and **members in particular.**"* 1 Cor. 12:27 (KJV)

If you are reading this book, you probably want to know and fulfill your prophetic destiny. Each and every one of us has not only a destiny, but also a particular ministry. Just as the body has eyes, ears, hands, backbone, lungs, heart, kidneys, legs, arms, and feet, every member has a part to play. Even if you feel you are just a microscopic cell in the body, you still have a part to play! Everyone has something to be and do to fulfill their destiny as a member of Christ's corporate Body/the Church.

Please accept and understand the truth that every person, every ministry, every organization, and every nation that is born of God has a destiny and purpose. If you have been born of God then you have a destiny. This ministry of which I am Bishop-apostolic overseer was born of God, and it has a destiny. There are nations, like Israel and others, that were born of God and that have a destiny.

The first step in birthing God's purpose is to have a revelation of what God has for us. So we want to discover who we are and what our purpose is in the Body of Christ and in God's divine destiny. A major part of the ministry of Christian International has been devoted to teaching and activating people in hearing the voice of God because we strongly believe in the power of prophecy to bring forth the purposes of God individually and corporately. In this book I describe corollary principles that will help transform a prophetic word or a God-given desire into a living reality.

The divine principle in Genesis is that every seed shall produce. How? *"According to its kind."* (Gen. 1:11, 25) Whatever family we were born into, we have the seed of that family. Our characteristic genetic heritage comes from our father and our mother. This principle is also true in the spirit realm. Everyone who has been born in this ministry or comes under the influence of this ministry will have the same seed.

The Destiny of God's Prophetic-Apostolic People

Several verses in Isaiah chapter 61 have special relevance to God's prophetic and apostolic people:

> *The Spirit of the Lord GOD is upon Me; because the LORD has anointed Me to preach good tidings to the poor; He has sent Me to heal the broken-hearted, to proclaim liberty to the captives, and the opening of the prison to those who are bound;* **To proclaim the acceptable year of the LORD,** *and the day of vengeance of our God; to comfort all who mourn.* (Isa. 61:1-2)

In this verse Isaiah wrote about the fact that we are to proclaim the acceptable year of the Lord. We need to know, and we can know, what time and season God has ordained in His divine purposes. The prophetic-apostolic people have been living in the time of the favor of the Lord and the acceptable year of the Lord for the last few years. Soon the day of vengeance of our God will come as the day of the Lord for executing His vengeance upon His enemies.

> *To console those who mourn in Zion, to give them beauty for ashes, the oil of joy for mourning, the garment of praise for the spirit of heaviness; that they may be called trees of righteousness, the planting of the LORD, that He may be glorified. **And they shall rebuild the old ruins,** they shall raise up the former desolations, and they shall repair the ruined cities, the desolations of many generations. (Isa. 61:3-4)*

This is a scripture that is very applicable to Christian International. We are re-builders, restorers of the old ruins. One of our major purposes is to bring restoration truths back into the Church which were lost during the Dark Ages.

> *Strangers shall stand and feed your flocks, and the sons of the foreigner shall be your plowmen and your vinedressers. But you shall be named the priests of the LORD: they shall call you the servants of our God. You shall eat the riches of the Gentiles, and in their glory you shall boast. Instead of your shame you shall have double*

honor; and instead of confusion they shall rejoice in their portion. Therefore in their land they shall possess double; everlasting joy shall be theirs. (Isa. 61:5-7)

One of our prophetic "Word of the Lord" messages for the year 2000 was the double portion. Double means multiplication.

"For I the LORD love justice; I hate robbery for burnt offering; I will direct their work in truth, and will make with them an everlasting covenant. **Their descendants shall be known among the Gentiles, and their offspring among the people. All who see them shall acknowledge them, that they are the posterity whom the LORD has blessed."** *I will greatly rejoice in the LORD, my soul shall be joyful in my God; for He has clothed me with the garments of salvation, He has covered me with the robe of righteousness, as a bridegroom decks himself with ornaments, and as a bride adorns herself with her jewels.* **For as the earth brings forth its bud, as the garden causes the things that are sown in it to spring forth, so the Lord GOD will cause righteousness and praise to spring forth before all the nations.** (Isa. 61:8-11)

The Holy Spirit spoke through Prophet Isaiah in terms of **seed, offspring, labor, and birthing** the purposes of God. Now let's look at Isaiah 66:7-11:

*"Before she was **in labor**, she gave **birth**; Before her pain came, she **delivered a male child.** Who*

*has heard such a thing? Who has seen such things? Shall the earth be made to give **birth** in one day? Or shall a nation be **born** at once? For as soon as **Zion was in labor**, she gave **birth** to her children. Shall I bring to the **time of birth**, and not cause **delivery**?" says the LORD. "Shall I who cause **delivery** shut up the **womb**?" says your God. "Rejoice with Jerusalem, and be glad with her, all you who love her; Rejoice for joy with her, all you who mourn for her; That you may feed and be satisfied with the consolation of her bosom, that you may drink deeply and be delighted with the abundance of her glory."*

Both of these prophetic scriptures are dualistic prophecies which means they have a natural application to Israel and the city of Jerusalem, as well as a spiritual application to the Church and individual ministries. If you are an apostolic-prophetic Christian you will find the revelation of your personal destiny within the context of God's purposes in His Body/Church today.

A Place Where the Principles of Birthing Are Practiced

Awhile back I asked God, "Lord, what is the real membership ministry of Christian International? What are we really called to do? What is our part in the Body of Christ?" He told me that we were a particular part of the Body that I hadn't quite related to before, but as He began to reveal it I understood its significance. I trust that by the time you have finished reading this book you will see and understand it too.

God revealed that Christian International's membership ministry is that of a **womb** in the Body of Christ. We are a place that conceives new truth in the womb of our spirit, bringing revelation and activation of new moves of God. We are a birthing center, a womb in the Body of Christ, the Church-Bride. Then we also have the responsibility of nurturing the new baby that God allows us to bring forth.

Another way this can be described is in terms of a chicken and an egg. (Since I grew up as an Oklahoma country boy, I often see spiritual truths in terms of farm life. Hopefully you city folk have seen these things on television so you will understand what I'm talking about.) We could say that CI is not only **an incubator for hatching eggs, we are a brooder house for growing them up into grown chickens.**

Some of you who are related to CI will become prophetic intercessors, like sitting hens that sit on the nest until the eggs hatch. Others will help grow to be "fryers." So, we're getting some of you ready to be cut into proper pieces to be cooked and served to the Body of Christ. The others will grow into sitting hens which will be put on the nest. There is much that needs to be done and all those associated with this ministry are definitely being prepared for something.

A Reproducing Anointing

Since Christian International is a place of conception and birthing, one of the great anointings that is upon this ministry is a "reproducing anointing." God made us to be reproducers of all that He has given to us. Because of this calling and anointing upon the founder and head of Christian International, all who are under this ministry receive of that anointing according to their fivefold calling, membership ministry, and destiny. If you come under this anointing and come under the influence of this ministry, then you are going to have a reproducing anointing.

I once asked the Lord, "What is my prophetic-apostolic anointing ability?" He said, "You are like the queen bee in the hive. You house the anointing to lay eggs of revelation that will bring forth the workers and warriors." My divine anointing and commission is to bring the revelation, understanding, and insight for what God is about to do in bringing restoration to the Church. This will be covered more in Chapter Six.

None of us appoint ourselves to a calling or endow ourselves with a divine anointing. This is strictly the sovereign choice of God. Christ Jesus wants us to enter into God's choice for us and to recognize, accept, and allow that anointing to accomplish the purpose for which it was given.

Raising up a Great Company of Apostles and Prophets

Christian International is called to raise up God's great company of prophets and apostles. Although we preach the whole fivefold ministry, our main commission is to call forth and help restore God's prophets and apostles. Our divine commission is to be a company of apostles and prophets demonstrating and establishing the ministry of prophets and apostles back into Christ's Church. We are to provide the revelation and activation that will produce a multitude of apostolic-prophetic ministers, apostolic-prophetic local churches, apostolic-prophetic ministers in the marketplace, and a great company of apostolic-prophetic saints.

When God spoke to me regarding this revelation truth and application of Malachi 4:5 (that God will send an Elijah company of prophets before the great "Day of the Lord"), as near as can be determined, I was the first one to receive it. I have had the privilege and challenge of pioneering these truths. In 1983 I wrote down this revelation and application in the book *Prophets and Personal Prophecy.* When God calls you to be a pioneer in bringing a truth forward you face great criticism. Even today when numerous ministries around the world are preaching these truths, the religious critics and unbelievers concerning present day prophets and prophetic ministry will still ridicule these statements. However, I still believe with all my heart that they are divinely accurate and scripturally sound. They are not just imaginations and theories, but prophetic revelations that have been proven in the lives of thousands to whom we have ministered this revelation and ministry.

We are fulfilling Malachi 4:5 as a company of apostles and prophets with the Elijah/John the Baptist anointing and ministry. We are a company that is called and ordained of God to prepare the way and make ready a people for the coming of the Lord. We believe according to New Testament teaching that the apostles along with the prophets have the calling and anointing to be counted among that company of Elijah/John the Baptist ministers called to fulfill prophecy.

Evidence of Spiritual Multiplication

Jesus told the religious Pharisees that if they could not believe His teaching alone, then they should believe because of the many proofs and confirmation of its accuracy by the works of His ministry (Jn. 10:38). Therefore, in addition to explaining the concept of a reproducing anointing, I give the following example to show its effectiveness.

In the first few decades of my ministry, I was the only one who prophesied. Then God gave me the vision to reproduce my anointing in others. After conceiving the revelation in my spirit for prophets and prophetic ministry to be restored to the Body of Christ, nurturing it through prayer, and waiting on the process of God, the revelation was birthed in me and I have had the challenge of bringing forth this "baby," along with the co-laborers the Lord has sovereignly brought. I'll describe this process in more detail later on; here I want to bring forth the point that since the Prophetic Movement was birthed in 1988, the process of conception and multiplication has continued.

As of this writing over 500 apostles, prophets, and apostolic-prophetic ministers belong to our Christian International Network of Churches (CINC). More than 200 churches are pastored by these ministers. Others are full-time traveling ministers or function in specialized ministries such as Prophetic Prayer Counseling. We have two Christian International headquarters in the United

States, plus headquarters in Europe, East Asia, Canada, Australia, South America, and India.

All of the ministers and saints trained by CI minister prophetically. Our traveling prophets have prophesied to thousands of individuals. Our apostolic-prophetic pastors with their prophetic teams have prophetically ministered to several thousand during the last decade. I know that during my 48 years of ministry over 40,000 have received personal prophecy through me. Prophets whom I have taught, trained, and activated such as Sharon Stone, John and Mary Webster, Scott and Kathy Webster, Tom and Jane Hamon, Buddy and Mary Crum, Steve Schultz, Tom and Diane Morrison, Glenn and Sherilyn Miller, Leon and Donna Walters, and others too numerous to mention at this time, have each prophesied to an average of more than a thousand individuals every year for the last 10 to 15 years.

Christian International Family Church here in Santa Rosa Beach, Florida has taught, trained, and equipped many prophetic teams. Every Friday night at our School of the Holy Spirit prophetic teams minister personal prophecy to around 130 people, averaging around 500 every month of the year. We also minister to all registered guests at each CI conference. Other CI churches have prophetic teams which minister every Friday night, such as Life Center in Atlanta, Georgia; Zion Family Church in Dallas, Texas; Baton Rouge Christian Center in Louisiana; and Christian International Family Worship Center in Versailles, Indiana, just to mention a few. Some of our individual prophets and prophetic churches provide prophetic ministry to several thousand individuals each year.

At that rate our 500 ministers and churches would each average ministering prophetically to 1,000 individuals annually. This is not taking into consideration the more than 30,000 saints and 6,000 ministers and church leaders that we have activated into prophetic ministry through the Manual for Ministering Spiritual Gifts, of whom many are not CINC ministers, nor the hundreds of students who have attended our Ministry Training College and received in-depth prophetic training.

One million would be a very conservative figure for the amount of people who have received personal prophecy from Christian International ministers, especially since the birthing of the Prophetic Movement in 1988. Every year it keeps increasing. This is not even including prophetic words over churches, cities, territories, and nations.

By taking the time to reproduce in others the gifting God gave me, far more people have been reached than if I had devoted my time to prophesying myself. One million is 25 times as many people receiving the word of the Lord in 10-15 years through CI ministers than Bill Hamon has ministered to in over 40 years. I continually encourage my spiritual children and grandchildren to do better, go farther, and reach higher in the things of God than I have.

Every one of these prophetic words that has been sent out is a divine seed to help someone fulfill prophetic destiny. If the seed lands in good soil, is nurtured and fed, and given the proper time to develop, it will come forth as a fully birthed purpose of God.

Chapter 3

SIX STEPS IN THE PROCESS OF BIRTHING GOD'S PURPOSE IN YOUR LIFE

How do you produce a purpose? How do you birth something? As Christian International has functioned as a womb in the Body of Christ, we have gone through the process of spiritual conception, pregnancy, and birthing. Although each birth is unique, there are certain crucial elements in the process that must be followed. I will list the steps below in conceiving, birthing, and maturing to fulfillment.

To illustrate this process let us use the natural example of a couple with the destiny to birth a child, who is destined to accomplish something that will bless the world. Some of you are single and some married, nevertheless, you understand the process of dating, marriage, and becoming parents. Our analogy will refer to an idealistic God-ordained married couple with the goal of birthing children. The child is like a move of God, a truth, or a revelation. In the subsequent chapters I will explain in more detail what this means to us spiritually.

1. First of all, we need to get a revelation of what God has for us.

In terms of our illustration, a couple who is dating needs to get a revelation of whether the other person is the one for them. The first step is to receive a revelation that they are for each other. They each have to come to an understanding that this one is for me, I am for this one, and we are for each other. We have a destiny together in God.

In the last chapter we discussed knowing our membership ministry and prophetic destiny--where we fit in the Body. One of the keys to discovering our personal place is finding out what God is doing corporately. When I learned God's heart to restore apostles and prophets as the pattern of Church govern-ment He established, God birthed this vision inside me and it became the focus of my personal ministry.

2. Secondly, you must make a covenant like a marriage vow to God that you will stay with His purpose and ministry regardless of the ways it may affect your life.

For a couple to produce a child according to God's will, they must first make a commitment to each other through a legally binding ceremony, a wedding. In God's divine purpose and order there can be no conception until there is first a proper commitment in marriage. That's the proper order. God wants a committed family structure in place to provide for the coming baby and raise it to adulthood.

God will not normally birth a revelation and get us pregnant with some truth until we first have a ceremony/covenant in which we commit ourselves to bring that "child" forth and then raise it to adulthood.

3. There is a conception. For conception to take place there must be an intimate relationship.

Usually a marriage starts out with a honeymoon so that the couple can have time alone with just each other. It is only when the couple is united that they can fulfill their destiny together of having a child.

In the next chapter we will look at Abraham who Scripture calls a prophet and friend of God. Through intimate relationship with God, He conceived and brought forth the natural nation of Israel and the spiritual truths of God's purposes and plans.

4. The pregnancy must be maintained by keeping faith and confidence in what we are pregnant with until it progresses to God's time for its birth.

The woman must carry the baby in her womb until the time of birthing. There is only one person who has the responsibility for the baby while it is being carried in the womb. Once it is born, everybody can help take care of the baby in many ways, but the one pregnant must be committed to carrying it until it is birthed. Sometimes she may get down to the seventh, eighth, or ninth month and think, "I want to back out." Too late! There must be no aborting the baby.

There came a time when Tim, Tom, and Sherilyn were all conceived and birthed by my wife and me. Evelyn did the hard work, but I had to make a living, provide the money, keep her clothed, fed, and all. It was hard! Evelyn carried them for nine months and, as short as she is, from three months on you would have thought she was going to give birth at any moment, and she wished she could have. She had to carry the boys for the full nine months, but only eight with Sherilyn, for she was born one month early.

In the spiritual arena the time period from conception to birthing can vary–it may be several years–nevertheless, we must persevere through all the doubt, persecution, and burden until God's set time. What signals that the time of pregnancy, the waiting time, is completed? The labor pains begin.

5. Labor pains.

Our daughter and two daughters-in-law had babies by natural birth at birthing centers. I remember when we were with our daughter, Sherilyn, while she was in labor and her husband Glenn was coaxing her along as he was trained in helping her breathe properly so that she could cooperate with the labor pains. An observer could have thought, "Why is she carrying on like that? Why is she making all those strange sounds and actions? I don't feel any pain." No, of course not. The one who is carrying the baby is the one who really feels the pain when the intense labor for birthing time comes.

The pregnant one must endure and not resist the labor pains but work with them until the baby is born. The time of labor and travail is the most dramatic, painful part of the process, but it is what pushes the new baby from the realm of faith into the realm of reality. The labor pains indicate something new is almost here, ready to come forth and be birthed!

6. **After the baby is born we are committed--dedicated to raising and maturing the child to fulfill its ministry and destiny.**

No responsible parent births a baby, gets excited, sends out birth announcements and photographs to all their friends, and then ignores the baby. The birth is just the beginning!

Likewise, each new purpose of God must be prayed and warred over, fed, nurtured, and protected as it grows into a living reality.

Before Wayne Williamson and Tonya King, my secretary and niece, decided to get married, they prayed, thought about it, and decided that they were for each other. Then they made a life commitment and said, "Okay, we believe we are to produce a child. We are to bring forth a new life. We are to produce a ministry together." They then set a date to legally make this a binding contract with each other and God. They acted upon their revelation, love, and conviction by committing themselves to each other in a legal ceremony on October 18, 1998. In 1999 Tonya became pregnant. She held in there throughout the nine months of her pregnancy and on March 31, 2000 she gave to birth to a son, Caleb. Now they are involved in the process of raising this baby, a process that will continue for many years to come.

These are six steps that must take place for conception, pregnancy, birthing, and maturing in the natural. We already looked at the first step in Chapter Two. Now we will see how the remaining principles apply to spiritual conception and multiplication.

Chapter 4

ABRAHAM
PROPHET AND FRIEND OF GOD

*"Surely the Lord **GOD does nothing,** unless He reveals*
*His **secret** to **His servants the prophets.**"* Amos 3:7

In the mid 1970's while I was flying on a plane God whispered in my spirit and said, "I called you to be an Abraham and your ministry will be like that of Abraham." That happened more than twenty years ago and I no longer remember from where to where I was going, but I still remember God speaking to me. At the time I did not fully grasp the implications of that statement.

I knew that in my family I was an Abraham, as I was the first in my family of seven to become a Christian. Over the next eight years I was instrumental in leading my two brothers, two sisters, mom, and dad to the Lord Jesus. I was the first to be born of the Spirit and the only one who went into full-time ministry, although my two brothers had a call into ministry. I was a pioneer then, even as I became the pioneer of the truth and practice of activating saints in the gifts of the Spirit--the Prophetic Movement. I am one of the pioneers teaching and practicing the apostolic and am now pioneering the way for the Saints Movement.

I am currently writing a book concerning the coming Saints Movement which will reveal more about this.

God's Covenant and Blessing

Now let us look more at our father of the faith and of the prophets to determine more ways to know and fulfill prophetic destiny. God birthed the entire Jewish race and the spiritual Church race through Father Abraham and his wife Sarah, so we can learn much about the principles of spiritual multiplication through him.

Abraham reveals many of the characteristics that a person needs in order to be a true prophet and friend of God. In a moment we will look at one particular incident in the life of Abraham that reveals the intimacy Abraham had with God which enabled him to conceive the purposes of God. But first let's address the second principle in birthing God's purpose: covenant.

> *Now the LORD had said to Abram: "Get out of your country, from your family and from your father's house, to the land that I will show you. I will make you a great nation; I will bless you and make your name great; and you shall be a blessing. I will bless those who bless you, and I will curse him who curses you; and in you all the families of the earth shall be blessed." So Abram departed as the Lord had spoken to him...* (Gen. 12:1-4)

Here we see God calling Abram and making a promise to him that his seed will be multiplied to become a mighty nation that will bless the entire world. Abram showed his willingness to enter into this covenant by obeying the Lord's requirement for him to leave his homeland and go to a new place. The similarity of this vow to the marriage covenant can be seen by the instruction to Abram to leave his father's household (see Gen. 2:24). Abram had to leave behind the old ways and be united in covenant to God's purpose.

An Encounter with the Lord

Most of you know the story of Abram's journeys and how God reestablished covenant with him, causing him to be circumcised, and changed his name to Abraham. Now let's read the details of an encounter he had with the Lord in Genesis 18:

> *Then the LORD appeared to him by the terebinth trees of Mamre, as he was sitting in the tent door in the heat of the day. So he lifted his eyes and looked, and behold, three men were standing by him; and when he saw them, he ran from the tent door to meet them, and bowed himself to the ground, and said, "My Lord, if I have now found favor in Your sight, do not pass on by Your servant. Please let a little water be brought, and wash your feet, and rest yourselves under the tree. And I will bring a morsel of bread, that you may refresh your hearts. After that you may pass by, inasmuch as you have come to your servant." They said, "Do as you have said." So Abraham hurried into the tent to Sarah and said, "Quickly, make ready three measures of fine meal; knead it and make cakes." And Abraham ran to the herd, took a tender and good calf, gave it to a young man, and he*

hastened to prepare it. So he took butter and milk and the calf which he had prepared, and set it before them; and he stood by them under the tree as they ate. Then they said to him, "Where is Sarah your wife?" And he said, "Here, in the tent." And He said, "I will certainly return to you according to the time of life, and behold, Sarah your wife shall have a son." (Sarah was listening in the tent door which was behind him.) Now Abraham and Sarah were old, well advanced in age; and Sarah had passed the age of childbearing. Therefore Sarah laughed within herself, saying, "After I have grown old, shall I have pleasure, my lord being old also?" And the LORD said to Abraham, "Why did Sarah laugh, saying, 'Shall I surely bear a child, since I am old?' Is anything too hard for the LORD? At the appointed time I will return to you, according to the time of life, and Sarah shall have a son." But Sarah denied it, saying, "I did not laugh," for she was afraid. And He said, "No, but you did laugh!" (v. 1-15)

Here we find that God sent three heavenly dignitaries on a secret assignment to reveal some of His secrets, times, and things He was about to do. Abraham called one of the three "Lord." They had a special message for Abraham concerning his and Sarah's prophetic destiny.

The Secrets of God

The Bible says in Genesis 20:7 that Abraham was a prophet. God had some secrets to reveal and fulfill, but He would do nothing until He revealed His secrets unto His prophet, Abraham.

Then the men rose from there and looked toward Sodom, and Abraham went with them to send them on the way. And the LORD said, "Shall I hide from Abraham what I am doing, since Abraham shall surely become a great and mighty nation, and all the nations of the earth shall be blessed in him? For I have known him, in order that he may command his children and his household after him, that they keep the way of the LORD, to do righteousness and justice, that the LORD may bring to Abraham what He has spoken to him." And the LORD said, "Because the outcry against Sodom and Gomorrah is great, and because their sin is very grave, I will go down now and see whether they have done altogether according to the outcry against it that has come to Me; and if not, I will know." (v. 16-21)

After the three dignitaries had revealed to Abraham that he and Sarah would have a child, the Lord took Abraham aside and revealed to him that He was heading down to Sodom and Gomorrah to utterly destroy them if their wickedness was as great as reported. The Lord had decided He wanted to go down and personally check out the reports that had been coming to Him that the towns of Sodom and Gomorrah were exceedingly wicked, becoming a terrible stench. The Creator of mankind wanted to see if they were as wicked as the pre-flood generation He had judged unworthy to remain on His earth. In that case He removed them by the Great Flood but used Noah to preserve the human race. It sounded like the Sodomites' cup of iniquity was full and running over.

They were no longer fit to stay alive and active on God's earth. The time of judgment was near at hand.

Prophetic Intercession

Then the men turned away from there and went toward Sodom, but Abraham still stood before the LORD. And Abraham came near and said, "Would You also destroy the righteous with the wicked? Suppose there were fifty righteous within the city; would You also destroy the place and not spare it for the fifty righteous that were in it? Far be it from You to do such a thing as this, to slay the righteous with the wicked, so that the righteous should be as the wicked; far be it from You! Shall not the Judge of all the earth do right?" (Only friends communicate in such a manner.) *So the LORD said, "If I find in Sodom fifty righteous within the city, then I will spare all the place for their sakes." Then Abraham answered and said, "Indeed now, I who am but dust and ashes have taken it upon myself to speak to the Lord: Suppose there were five less than the fifty righteous; would You destroy all of the city for lack of five?" So He said, "If I find there forty-five, I will not destroy it." And he spoke to Him yet again and said, "Suppose there should be forty found there?" So He said, "I will not do it for the sake of forty." Then he said, "Let not the Lord be angry, and I will speak: Suppose thirty should be found there?" So He said, "I will not do it if I find thirty there." And he said, "Indeed now, I have taken it upon myself to speak to the Lord: Suppose twenty should be found there?" So He*

said, "I will not destroy it for the sake of twenty."
Then he said, "Let not the Lord be angry, and I will
speak but once more: Suppose ten should be found
there?" And He said, "I will not destroy it for the
sake of ten." So the LORD went His way as soon
as He had finished speaking with Abraham; and
Abraham returned to his place.(v. 22-33)

Abraham started interceding. He said, "My nephew and his family live in Sodom. If you rain fire and brimstone down upon them, Lot and his family will die also. Could you spare them?" Abraham began to engage in what could be called **prophetic intercession**. He started out asking about 50 righteous people, then 45 and on down until he finally said, "Now God, don't get upset at me, don't get angry at me, but if you can just find 10 righteous people out of the whole big city would you spare it?" God answered Abraham, "If I can find 10 people that are righteous I will spare it." But God could not find enough righteous people, so He destroyed the city completely. Yet He was merciful to Lot because of Abraham's intercession. He sent an angel and brought Lot, his wife, and their two daughters out before destruction rained down upon the cities. As you know, Lot's wife looked back and turned into a pillar of salt. The daughters and Lot escaped, and the rest of the inhabitants of Sodom and Gomorrah became "crispy critters."

A Prophet and Friend of God

Notice the major reasons God gave for revealing His secrets to Abraham. God revealed His secrets to Abraham because he was a PROPHET and also a FRIEND of God.

God said, "Abraham, because I know you will discipline your children to keep the way of the Lord and do righteousness and justice, I'm going to reveal to you some of My secrets. Because you are destined not only to be a great nation but the father of many nations, and because you have demonstrated obedience and faithfulness I'm going to now multiply your seed and use you to fulfill destiny." Abraham was in covenant with God and shared intimacy with Him, so God birthed His purposes through him. God multiplied his seed and Abraham fulfilled his prophetic destiny.

A master does not communicate to his servants all that he is planning on doing and fulfilling. But to his friends he does. Jesus declared in John 15:14-15, 26-27:

> *You are My FRIENDS if you do whatever I command you. No longer do I call you servants, for a servant does not know what his master is doing; but **I have called you friends, for all things that I heard from My Father I have made known to you**...But when the Helper comes, whom I shall send to you from the Father, **the Spirit of truth** who proceeds from the Father, **He will testify** of Me. And you also will bear witness, because you have been with Me from the beginning.*

He said, "I'm going to send My Holy Spirit and He's going to reveal things to you." The Apostle John was an intimate friend of Jesus and God shared profound secrets with him in his Revelation.

Then he (an angel) *said to me, "Write: 'Blessed are those who are called to the marriage supper of the Lamb!'" And he said to me, "These are the true sayings of God." And I fell at his feet to worship him. But he said to me, "See that you do not do that! I am your fellow servant, and of your brethren who have the testimony of Jesus. Worship God! For the testimony of Jesus is the spirit of prophecy."* (Rev. 19:9-10)

Those who are called to the marriage supper of the Lamb are intimate with God. They know His true sayings and have the testimony of Jesus--the spirit of prophecy. This is why it is so important that prophecy and prophetic ministry be fully restored to the Church. We can be a friend of God like Abraham. We can know the things of God. We're called to be friends of God and know what God is doing and about to do.

Chapter 5

THE KEYS OF DAVID

"The key of the house of David I will lay on his shoulder;
So he shall open, and no one shall shut; And he shall shut,
and no one shall open." Isa. 22:22

In the mid-1970's I received prophecies stating that God was giving me several keys of different colors and shapes. These were special keys for unlocking the treasures of heaven, to unlock doors of truth that had been shut for centuries and that would bring restoration of truth into His Church. God also revealed to me when I was a single pastor at the age of 20 that my life would follow the pattern of David's life. He would establish for me a house of Hamon to leave a heritage for my descendants as the house of David left a divine destiny for his descendants.

Our Eschatology Influences Our
Interpretation of Prophecy

This revelation did not make a lot of sense to me at the time for I believed so strongly in the imminent return of Christ that I was convinced that Jesus would probably come before I was able to marry and have children. So I figured it must be talking about going to heaven and having a mansion there. It is amazing how our eschatological beliefs can hinder us from grasping prophetic revelation from the heart and mind of God.

As a young zealous preacher I wanted to see instant results in my ministry for I thought the time was very short. But Father God took his young son through His processes of maturing and preparation. Many of you have heard me tell how I became so frustrated as a young minister that I prayed to die. God said, "It's about time! I've been waiting for you to allow Me to kill off Bill Hamon's flesh so that I can use you to show forth My Son Jesus." Throughout these processes, the seeds of the prophetic words, of my prophetic destiny, were germinating within me, waiting until the maturing process had progressed enough to bring each one forward.

The Key of the Prophet - Revelation Knowledge

Over the years God has given us revelation keys of the kingdom to open the door to activating saints in their gifts of the Spirit, in prophetic ministry, in apostolic ministry, and as ministers in the marketplace. One of the keys is the "Key of David." I believe Isaiah 22:22 is personally applicable to all of God's prophetic and apostolic people, as well as to me and to Christian International.

On the day of Pentecost Peter said:

*"Brothers, I can tell you confidently that the patriarch David died and was buried, and his tomb is here to this day. But **he was a prophet,** and knew that God had promised him on oath that he would place one of his descendants on his throne."* (Acts 2:29-30 NIV)

Just as Abraham was a prophet and friend to God, so God called David a prophet and a man after His own heart (Acts 13:22).

When we accepted God's mandate to pioneer the revelation and activation of God's great company of prophets, the Lord reminded me about the prophecies concerning "keys." He said, "I am now giving you one of the keys to the house of David." The key was to the door of David's room as a prophet.

For years we have been using that particular "key of the house of David." Now there are other scriptures that speak of the key of David that will make a personal application to our situation. There is a greater revelation in God's declaration, "I will open doors. I will open and shut, and no man can open what I shut and no man can shut what I open." (See Rev. 3:7-9)

Let us look at what Jesus said about prophets and apostles in Luke 11:49-52:

> *Therefore the wisdom of God also said,* ***"I will send them prophets and apostles, and some of them they will kill and persecute,*** *that the blood of all the prophets* ***which was shed from the foundation of the world may be required of this generation,*** *from the blood of Abel to the blood of Zechariah who perished between the altar and the temple. Yes, I say to you, it shall be required of this generation. Woe to you lawyers! For you have taken away* ***the key of knowledge.*** *You did not enter in yourselves, and those who were entering in you hindered."*

Persecution and Killing

Since we are a prophetic-apostolic company we have only two options from the old order Pharisee leaders–being persecuted or killed. If you are being persecuted and killed you are probably in the apostolic-prophetic company!

Jesus said that He would send prophets and apostles and that they would be the "keys of revelation knowledge." It is true in our time as it was then: the established old order religious leaders think they are the standard and determining factor for all acceptable Christian teaching and practice. Like the Pharisees they reject prophets and apostles, won't go in the open door themselves, and try to shut the door to prevent other people from following the revelation knowledge that prophets and apostles bring. Jesus said, "Because of that I'm going to bring all My wrath and the judgment I have for those who have killed My prophets down through the centuries and pour it out on one generation." (see also Mt. 23:31-36) That word was to the generation which was alive when the ministries of Prophet John the Baptist and Prophet Jesus, the Son of God, were being manifest.

Now we are in the last generation of apostles and prophets being restored. The wisdom of God still declares that those who reject **God's present day prophets and apostles** will receive the judgments God has decreed against all those who have ever killed, rejected, or slandered God's holy apostles and prophets. This includes those who martyr and condemn apostles and prophets by speaking or writing books against them, not just those who murder them physically. People need to realize that it is no small matter to reject God's apostles and prophets. I can assure you that you do not want to be a part of the generation that rejects God's apostles and prophets.

Do Not Shut What God Wants Revealed

Somebody gave me a book not long ago written by one of those self-appointed critics who think they are the sheriffs in the Body of Christ and the final authority for all truth and Christian experiences. The author quoted from books by major leaders in the Charismatic, Faith, and Prophetic Movements. I think he quoted from one of my books in almost every chapter.

In one place he wrote that "Hamon" (these type of writers give no recognition to anyone as Dr., Bishop, Prophet, Pastor, or Apostle) said if anybody rejects God's prophets they are actually rejecting God. Then he added his own statement, that Hamon believes and teaches that anybody who rejects him rejects God, which he followed by accusing me of being presumptuous and putting myself as equal with God.

Well, as a human being I'm just another man, but if I am truly representing the Lord Jesus and speaking His words as one of God's anointed prophets, then Bill Hamon is nothing, but Jesus Christ ministering His words through one of His prophets is everything. These critics do not believe that God has real prophets who speak His words today. But God's written Word declares that Jesus gave some to be prophets and apostles and God set apostles and prophets in His Church to function as long as His Church is on planet earth. (Eph. 4:11; 1 Cor. 12:28)

In her book *The Next Move of God* Dr. Fuchsia Pickett wrote:

> God spoke a startling message to me one night as I was ministering in a church in North Carolina. He declared: "I will not, I will not, I will not allow anyone who touches My plan, My program, My prophets or My prophecy to be a part of, or participate in, the next move of God." I immediately recognized the book of Jude in outline form in that statement. He had mentioned four of the seven steps that led the Church into apostasy. I realized that there are sins committed against God that are much worse than sins we commit against our fellow man. It is not a light matter to be involved in criticism or betrayal of an anointed servant of God.[1]

When Jesus was ministering as God's Prophet and only begotten Son on earth He told the religious leaders who were rejecting Him and His words that they were actually rejecting the very God that they claimed to believe in and serve. Jesus declared that He was not representing Himself or speaking His own words but those of His heavenly Father, Jehovah God. If an apostle or prophet is truly representing Jesus Christ and speaking God's pure words, then those who reject and seek to make null and void those words are in all reality rejecting Jesus Christ. When Israel rejected Prophet Samuel's prophecies and ministry, God made this very revealing statement, *"They have not rejected you, but they have rejected Me, that I should not reign over them."* (1 Sam. 8:7)

---

[1]Fuchsia Pickett, *The Next Move of God,* Creation House, 1994, p. 61.

I am not speaking about not following scriptures which speak of testing ministers and teachings to make sure they are of God. I am speaking of those who speak against God's true apostles and prophets from the same motivation that the Pharisees had when they spoke against the apostles and prophets of the first century New Testament Church.

Jesus loves His holy and true apostles and prophets for they are preparing the way and making ready a people for His second coming. Jesus wants to come back. He wants to take over His creation. He intensely desires to establish His righteous kingdom over all the earth. If He wanted to do it alone or with His angels He would have done it long ago. But He wants to do it in, with, and through His Church. All leaders who hinder those who are co-laboring with Christ to bring about His purpose will be dealt with severely by Him. In all reality it has nothing to do with you or me, it has to do with Christ's divine purpose for His Church.

An Open Door

Let us look at one more scripture on the **Key of David:**

*And to the angel of the church in Philadelphia write, "These things says He who is holy, He who is true, **'He who has the key of David, He who opens and no one shuts, and shuts and no one opens:** I know your works. See, I have set before you an open door, and no one can shut it; for you have a little strength, have kept My word, and have not denied My name.'"* (Rev. 3:7-9)

In this letter Jesus revealed Himself as the One who has the key of David. We are a Philadelphia church ministry with the key of David. This key opens the doors of revelation of the mysteries of Christ and the next moves of God. The apostles and prophets are the gatekeepers with the keys to open and shut. We can possess the gates of our enemies, as was promised to Abraham. No matter how much opposition may come against us, we must overcome and not abort the purposes of God.

Chapter 6

UNDERSTANDING AND FULFILLING GOD'S TIMES FOR BIRTHING

"Of the children of Issachar who had understanding of the times, to know what Israel ought to do, their chiefs were two hundred; and all their brethren were at their command." 1 Chr. 12:32

There are servants of the Lord who have the anointing to see in the Spirit and in the Scriptures what God is about to do. This enables them to understand God's divine times, seasons, and purposes.

The Sons of Issachar Anointing

Several prophecies have come over me that I have the anointing of the sons of Issachar. The sons of Issachar had a special anointing from God, a special grace, a special wisdom, and a special prophetic insight to know the times and seasons concerning what God's people ought to do. They were a special group who had this anointing, "and all their brethren were at their command." There were only 200 sons of Issachar out of the 340,000 warriors that came from the Israeli tribes to make David king over all Israel. That is less than one percent of the total of all the warriors that came from the tribes to establish the Davidic kingdom.

If the same percentage holds true in the Church as in Israel, there are less than one percent from among the thousands of ministers in the Church who have this special "sons of Issachar anointing" which enables them to know what God is about to do, to know His restoration movements and destiny for the Church. All prophets and apostles in the New Testament have this anointing to some degree, but only a small percentage of this group have the particular anointing to understand the "times of refreshing" and "times of restoration" in God's times and seasons.

> *...the mystery of Christ, which in other ages was not made known to the sons of men, as it has now been **revealed by the Spirit to His holy apostles and prophets.*** (Eph. 3:5)

The mysteries concerning the purposes and times of God and the Issachar anointing are transferred to both prophets and apostles. They have the anointing to know the seasons and the mysteries that are hidden in the Scriptures and to make this revelation known to the Body.

A Definite Prophetic Time

Daniel also had the God-given ability to discern the times he lived in.

> *In the first year of his* (Darius') *reign I, Daniel, understood by the books the number of the years specified by the word of the LORD through Jeremiah the prophet, that He would accomplish seventy years in the desolations of Jerusalem.* (Dan. 9:2)

Daniel had been reading the scripture in Jeremiah 29:10-14:

For thus says the LORD: **After seventy years are completed** *at Babylon, I will visit you and perform My good word toward you, and cause you to return to this place. For I know the thoughts that I think toward you, says the LORD, thoughts of peace and not of evil, to give you a future and a hope. Then you will call upon Me and go and pray to Me, and I will listen to you. And you will seek Me and find Me, when you search for Me with all your heart. I will be found by you, says the LORD, and I will bring you back from your captivity; I will gather you from all the nations and from all the places where I have driven you, says the LORD, and I will bring you to the place from which I caused you to be carried away captive.*

Seventy years were determined for the period of time of Israel's captivity in Babylon. There are very few places in the Bible where prophecy gives a specific time period. One is the 400 years that Abraham's seed was in Egypt and another is this 70-year period of Israel's Babylonian Captivity. God had said through Jeremiah that within 70 years He would restore Israel back to their homeland. Daniel was reading the book of Jeremiah and this prophetic word was illuminated to him. He probably exclaimed, "Praise God! Look at that!" Daniel went to the record books and calendar and determined that Israel had been in Babylon 70 years. He probably leapt and shouted, "Hallelujah! That 70 years is up. It's time for restoration to our homeland. The time is now!"

What to Do When the Time is Now

What are we to do when revelation comes that it is the appointed time for a prophecy to be fulfilled? Should we sit back and say, "Well, let's see if the prophet's word is going to come to pass?" Should we begin to scrutinize and analyze the prophecy to see if it really means what it says? Should we just say, "If it is really a true prophecy it will come to pass" but do nothing on our part to work for its fulfillment? Let's look at what Daniel did.

> *Then I set my face toward the Lord God to make request by prayer and supplications, with fasting, sackcloth, and ashes.* (Dan. 9:3)

When it is time to bring forth prophetic purpose and destiny then prophetic intercessors must come forth. When it is time for birthing, time for bringing forth, there must be intercessors. We need to intercede. When we understand that it is God's predetermined time for it to happen, then we need to make intercession and go into travail to bring it forth. Daniel humbled himself in sackcloth and ashes and went into a time of prayer and supplication with fasting to make request for God's time of restoration to take place.

The next verse says,

> *And I prayed to the LORD my God, and made confession, and said, "O Lord, great and awesome God, who keeps His covenant and mercy with those who love Him, and with those who keep His commandments, we have sinned and committed*

*iniquity, we have done wickedly and rebelled, even by departing from Your precepts and Your judgments. Neither have we heeded Your servants the **prophets**, who spoke in Your name to our kings and our princes, to our fathers and all the people of the land."* (Dan. 9:4-5)

Verse 4 reveals the two requirements for God to keep His covenant and mercy with us. We must love Him and keep His commandments. The Apostle Paul declared,

God will make all things work together for the good of those who love God and are called according to His purpose. (Rom. 8:28)

We must confess our sins and failures and admit where we have failed to keep all of God's commandments and covenants. Remember that Daniel was not confessing his own sins and shortcomings but those of the nation of Israel. Many leaders today will have to repent and confess, "We have not listened and responded properly to Your servants the **prophets,** who have spoken to us in Your Name." We must be willing to identify with the need and intercede for restoration.

*"We have not obeyed the voice of the LORD our God, **to walk in His laws,** which He set before us **by His servants the prophets**. Yes, all Israel has transgressed Your law, and has departed so as not to obey Your voice; therefore the curse and the oath written in the Law of Moses the servant of God have been poured out on us, because we have sinned against Him."* (Dan. 9:10)

If you read the whole prayer down to the end of the chapter, you will find that Daniel interceded and cried out to God for restoration. He was a prophet who had a sensitivity to the times and purposes of God. He prophesied about four great empires that were going to rule the world at different times over the next several centuries. He prophesied about the coming of Jesus, the Messiah. He prophesied about the Saints Movement that will take place in the last days, resulting in God's kingdom being established over all the earth. He saw the times and seasons of God. He received this insight through dreams, revelation by the Spirit, and illumination of the Scriptures. We need to believe for God to give us revelation as we read the Scriptures.

How to Know and Fulfill a God-Ordained Kairos Time

Most ministers know that the word translated "time" in the English Bible comes from two different Greek words: *kairos* and *chronos*. *Chronos* time means the ordinary passing of time. It is just regular time such as we measure through clocks and calendars. *Kairos* refers to a time of fulfillment or fullness of something, rather than a set date. In the birthing process *chronos* time is the time of conception and pregnancy up until the labor pains begin. Once a human baby is conceived there is an approximately nine month process of development in the womb. Using *chronos* time a due date can be estimated, but it may not be correct. When the labor pains come, then it is *kairos* time. That is the time of delivery, the time of birthing, the time of coming forth.

God rarely gives a specific *chronos* date to correspond with the *kairos* time of fulfillment of His word to us. So how does one know when it is a *kairos* time? First we receive a revelation of God's timing. Then we enter into intercession until we become so involved in what God is doing that we get on God's timetable. We labor in prayer and travail until we sense His *kairos* time has come. God's purpose is birthed at a *kairos* time by intercession.

At Christian International's 1996 "International Gathering of Apostles and Prophets" conference, Cindy Jacobs, who is head of Generals of Intercession, was the speaker. The Holy Spirit sovereignly moved and had us join together in a symbolic marriage of the prophets with the intercessors and the intercession ministry with the prophetic ministry. We felt it was necessary to have a full-time minister of intercession so we brought Martha Lucia on staff to head up, inspire, motivate, maintain, and mature our ministry of intercession. It has taken three years to arrive at our present status. We started out with around three faithfully committed intercessors, then grew to 30, and we hope soon to have 300.

We are now, and will become more and more, an apostolic-prophetic intercession church and ministry because we sense a *kairos* time coming soon. Christian International is getting ready to birth something again. We are getting ready to come into something like never before. God is going to raise up more and more intercessors. We are coming to a *kairos* time and the prophetic intercessors are the nurses and midwives to help bring forth the baby. I pray that everyone who reads this will be prepared for the soon to come *kairos* time.

Some Biblical Examples of Those Who Participated in a *Kairos* Time

Hannah prayed and interceded until she was able to birth Samuel, who was the one who brought forth the great company of prophets. Samuel was the father of the prophets. Prior to this Abraham and Moses were called prophets, but there wasn't a great number of prophets until Samuel came along and started the School of Prophets. Hannah became consumed with a desire to bear a child. She prayed with deep intercession, crying out to God until even the religious priest thought she was drunk. But she was desperate. There is a time to get desperate before God if you are going to birth something God wants brought forth.

Elijah discerned that it was time for the drought in Israel to be over. It had been going on for three years already and he sensed the time had come for it to end--a *kairos* time. He went up to Mount Carmel, demonstrated the power of God, killed all the false prophets, and then went into intercession. He stayed in prayer until he saw the hand of God extended by the sign of the cloud and until he knew in his spirit and had outward confirmation that the outpouring of rain was coming. He then arose and began to move on in God's purpose for his life. It takes intercession to birth an outpouring.

As we have seen, **Daniel** travailed in prayer to see Jeremiah's prophecy fulfilled for the restoration of Israel back to their homeland. We can know the times and seasons as Daniel knew them.

Jesus travailed in the Garden of Gethsemane for the birthing of His Church through His death, burial, resurrection, and the outpouring of His Holy Spirit. The Garden of Gethsemane is where He travailed, where He brought it forth. He paid the price through Calvary. He authorized His Church by His resurrection, birthed it, and empowered it with His Spirit on the day of Pentecost. It was the travail in the Garden that made the way and prepared Christ for the final labor pains on the cross and then the birthing of His Church on the Day of Pentecost. For the last 2,000 years Christ's Church has continued to multiply and the greatest harvest is yet to come!

A Biblical Symbolic Illustration of
Labor Pains and Birthing

*Now a great sign appeared in heaven: a woman clothed with the sun, with the moon under her feet, and on her head a garland of twelve stars. **Then being with child, she cried out in labor and in pain to give birth.** And another sign appeared in heaven: behold, a great, fiery red dragon having seven heads and ten horns, and seven diadems on his heads. His tail drew a third of the stars of heaven and threw them to the earth. And the dragon stood before the woman who was ready to give birth, to devour her child as soon as it was born. **She bore a male child who was to rule all nations with a rod of iron.** And her child was caught up to God and His throne.* (Rev. 12:1-5)

Here we have the symbolic description of a pregnant woman clothed with the sun, the moon under her feet, and a crown of twelve stars on her head. She was crying out in travailing labor pains to give birth. She bore a male child who was to rule all nations with a rod of iron. All of these Biblical examples confirm that there is a time of travail and there is a time of birthing.

The Value of Staying in Your Place of Preparation Until Time for Birth

I want to say one more thing regarding timing. To try to force birthing before the proper time always causes problems. Sometimes, for some reason, even a full-term birthing takes place without everything being completed as it should have been.

My grandson, Jason, who was born with a double cleft lip and palate, is a living illustration concerning the necessity of remaining in the place of God's preparation process until everything is finished. Medical experts say that the mouth area is the last part of a baby's head to make its final formation before birth. In Jason's case that area did not reach perfection before birthing. The process was not completed. Jason had to have several surgeries from the time he was five months old until he was four years old. They then waited until he grew to the age of twelve.

Recently the doctors did a four hour surgery. They performed an operation taking bone from his hip to join together the two gaps in his upper front jaw. It has taken all of these operations and will require several more to finish his lips, hard palate, and soft palate to bring his mouth and nose to the condition that they should have been in when he was born. It has been much more trouble after he was born to fix what should have been finished in the womb. It has taken hours of time for the parents, thousands of dollars in medical bills, and much trauma, pain, and suffering for Jason.

I have seen people who were in the womb of preparation in Bible college, in a church, in ministry, and in God's place of preparation and maturity. Some get anxious and impatient in trying to convince themselves that they are ready and properly prepared to be birthed into their ministry. Some even become convinced that God is telling them to launch. As the old saying goes, "They just got up and went without being properly and timely sent." Some launch into traveling ministry and others start their own church or non-profit ministry. They force a premature birth before many areas of their preparation have been completed.

Those who leave their place of preparation before the process is finished go through trauma after trauma and have to have spiritual operation after operation to try to finish what should have been done in the womb of preparation. Make sure you stay in God's place of preparation until the preparation process is complete, as God knows it should be.

Chapter 7

A PRESENT DAY ILLUSTRATION OF SPIRITUAL CONCEPTION AND BIRTHING OF A RESTORATION TRUTH

Now I want to give you a little history of Christian International, where we have come from, where we are in the present, and where we are going. As I have said, Christian International functions as a womb in the Body of Christ. God has given us the honor of functioning as a conception center, as a place where prophetic understanding and apostolic revelation is received. It is a place where new moves and purposes of God are birthed. If you have read *Prophets and the Prophetic Movement* you may be familiar with some of this history, but I am also including some details of events which have transpired since that writing.[1]

Conception Takes Place

In 1983 I had a revelation conception from God and got pregnant with the "Prophetic Movement" and the company of prophets that God was going to bring forth. When that happened I started writing my first book on prophecy, *Prophets and Personal Prophecy*. I wrote from

---

[1] *Prophets and the Prophetic Movement,* pp. 94-95.

1983 to 1986 and then it was published in September 1987. It is now in its tenth printing, totaling 147,000 copies, not including the copies translated into eight different languages which have gone to most of the nations in the world.

Our beginning labor pains came at CI's first International Gathering of the Prophets conference held near Destin, Florida in October 1987. (It became an annual conference and a few years later we began including Apostles in the title as well.) As far as I can determine by historical research, it was the first international prophets conference ever conducted in the history of the Church. Over 700 people attended this gathering. On Friday October 23, 1987, the third night of the conference, God moved with a sovereign sweep of His Spirit at 10:00 p.m. in the evening. A spirit of intercessory warfare praise and prayer arose spontaneously within all the people. For the next 45 minutes there was heavenly warfare/praise/prayer in the Spirit like few have ever witnessed. We went into spiritual labor pains. I am telling you the labor pains came heavily upon us. Some of those reading this may have been there. Visions and prophecies were given by many of those present revealing what had just transpired. The main emphasis of the words given was that the battle had been won for the release and activation of the great company of prophets that God had pre-ordained to be raised up in this century and even at this very time.

Although we had labor pains in 1987, we did not have birthing until 1988. We were pregnant with this ministry for quite some time. When a woman is pregnant with a baby she carries it nine months. When a man or woman of God is pregnant with a vision that is destined to become a restoration movement in the Church, they may carry it for years. Labor pains can begin one year without the birth taking place until years later. The sovereign move of God in that service was the preliminary labor pain that placed the baby, the Prophetic Movement, in the proper position along the birth canal for delivery the following year.

The Birth of the Prophetic Movement

One year later, we held the second CI Network of Prophetic Ministries International Prophets Conference. On October 15, 1988, the third night of the conference, there came a sovereign move of the Holy Spirit. At 10:15 p.m., when I had finished preaching on God's purpose for His great company of prophets being brought forth, a spirit of travail arose within me and a mighty anointing swept over me, as I began to travail in spiritual birth. The same spirit swept throughout the audience of over 800 people. For the next 50 minutes most of us travailed in prophetic intercessory prayer.

Have you ever had intercessory prayer hit you? It is like a woman in the last labor pains just before giving birth. As we cried out in the travail of birth pains the intercession intensified in my spirit until I felt my soul was being torn out. I almost physically passed out from the intensity of the anointing and spiritual birth pains. Finally, my whole body felt as weak as water, as if my very life was going out of me. I crumpled to my knees and was immediately caught up in the Spirit. I then saw a vision of

God lifting me and many others to a higher realm. He gave me a vision of the thousands of prophets He was bringing forth at that time.

A New Baby

This company of prophets was in the hand of God like a baby, which had just been brought from the womb. He asked if I would be one of those who would help raise up what He had birthed. He stated that a new anointing and authority had been granted for this purpose, and that all who were there and all those around the world who had received His vision for the company of prophets would receive this same anointing. As I ascended up with Him in the Spirit, all those present also ascended and began to form into a structure that would propagate the prophetic. I looked and saw other structures arising all across the world. He said this was the structure He had given me and that the others were many other prophetic groups that He was raising up. I was to work to help bring unity, relationship, and a networking among the different camps of prophets.

This vision has come to pass and is currently continuing to be fulfilled. Christian International has already been used by God to touch approximately one million people prophetically. But with over one half billion people currently in the Body of Christ worldwide, other camps are needed to complete the work of raising the Prophetic Movement to its full size, stature, and maturity. When I began giving personal prophecies over 45 years ago, I was one of the first to operate in this type of ministry. Pioneers often face more jeers than cheers.

Since that time I have rejoiced to see others be raised up in the Body of Christ who are teaching the same truths that God revealed to me. I am working together with many other apostles and prophets in the Church and the ministry structures which they represent to proclaim the truths of the Prophetic Movement throughout the world.

God revealed other things that night, as well as His purpose for the prophets. But mainly I want you to know that there was a birthing. There was a coming forth of the prophetic at that time. That was 1988, twelve years ago.

Another Conception

I said previously that I, and Christian International, function as a womb in the Body of Christ. It has been consistent that our International Gathering of Apostles and Prophets has served as the birthing center. We have had both conception and birth take place at these conferences. At the 1992 conference we had four guest speakers from Malaysia, Mexico, Canada, and the United States. These four major apostles and prophets, none of whom were CI ordained ministers, spoke unanimously that conception of the apostolic had taken place within Christian International.

Then in 1994 labor pains came, as well as my full acceptance of Christ's commission to be one of His apostles. Although I had functioned in the roles of pastor, evangelist, teacher, and head of a ministry organization, I had always seen myself in the office of a prophet because this was clearly the primary place of my anointing and revelation. Therefore, for many years I resisted the title of "apostle" even though I had received about 25 prophecies from others during the last 20 years about the calling of an apostle. By 1994, after being pregnant with God's vision for the Apostolic Movement, I acknowledged that He was calling me to function as an apostle as well. His anointing was upon me and CI to raise up a company of apostles, just as we had a company of prophets.

During the period of 1994 to 1996 CI made the transition from being mainly prophetic to being equally apostolic, and from just trying to bless people and bring revelation, to establishing and building people into the very structure that God wants the Church to be. Christian International Network of Churches (CINC) was structured to incorporate all that God has revealed and activated within me as Bishop and all of the Christian International ministries. The CINC local churches and pastors are the foundation and core ministry for fulfilling the vision for the full restoration of apostles and prophets and producing apostolic-prophetic local churches full of apostolic-prophetic people. The Christian International Business Network (CIBN) was established to raise up and fulfill the vision of providing the revelation that there are apostolic-prophetic ministers in the marketplace. Preparation has been made through trained personnel, materials, and local church chapters to bring the CIBN to maturity and worldwide ministry. In 1996 I started writing the book *Apostles, Prophets and the Coming Moves of God* which was published in 1997 and continues to be circulated throughout the Body of Christ.

Birthing the Apostolic

In October 1998 at the International Gathering, there was a birthing of the Apostolic Movement for Christian International. At this point I don't know how much of the rest of the Body of Christ it will affect, but like Joshua said, "As for me and my house" (Jos. 24:15) the Apostolic Movement was birthed.

The birthing came on this order. On Wednesday night of the conference, Dutch Sheets preached a message on the Father's heart of God. At the end of the message he asked me as the Apostolic Father of the ministry to come and release the heart of Father God to the ministers and saints present. At the end of my praying the spirit of intercession gripped me and I went to my knees and stayed there in intercessory prayer for around 30 minutes.

During the intercession I had a vision of Jesus coming to me with a big fiery glowing heart in His hands. It was as big as a basketball but shaped like a heart. Jesus came up to me and placed His Father's heart right into my chest cavity. My heart melted within me as His heart was given to me. I wept from a heart of gratitude and the tremendous sense of God's love and care. He impressed upon me that He was giving me His Father's heart to father His apostles as I had fathered His prophets. While God was speaking to me on the floor, Apostle Dutch Sheets was walking back and forth declaring that the apostolic was being birthed that night in our midst.

More to Come

At the International Gathering in 1999, Prophetess Cindy Jacobs was one of the guest speakers. During her evening of ministry we had a mighty move of the Holy Spirit. Corporate intercession was made for several nations as the Holy Spirit directed. Around 1,500 people were in attendance and almost everyone participated. She spoke under divine inspiration by revelation that something new had transpired in the heavenlies. The Saints Movement was conceived into the womb of Christian International at that time.

We are now definitely pregnant with the Saints Movement. We will carry it in the womb of our spirit, nurturing it by preaching about it and writing books and materials about it. We will lay the foundation for it in Scripture, prepare the people, and make a way for the coming of the Saints Movement. We will continue this pregnancy in God's *chronos* time until God's *kairos* time comes for the full birthing of the Saints Movement.

In the meantime we have our family of ministry responsibilities and divine commissioning, which has grown over the years, to maintain and parent until each "child" reaches maturity. As of this writing, we have a twelve year old Prophetic Movement, a two year old Apostolic Movement, and we are pregnant with the Saints Movement. We will cover the process of parenting more than one "child" in the next chapter.

One Part of the Body

This history has been given not to glorify CI, but rather as a testimony to what God has done. As stated at the outset, we know that we are just one small part of the hundreds of ministries and individual members of the Body of Christ that are being used of God to fulfill His purpose. All of the parts of the Body can use these principles to birth something that Christ Jesus wants brought forth into their personal life, local church, or the corporate Body of Christ. Any willing believer can position him or herself to birth and multiply God's purpose.

Chapter 8

PARENTING THE PURPOSES OF GOD

"The things that you have heard from me among many witnesses, commit these to faithful men who will be able to teach others also." 2 Tim. 2:2

Raising the Baby to Maturity

Since the primary subject of this book is birthing God's purpose, I will not go into a lot of detail here on the process of raising to maturity. However, it is crucial to understand that if we want God to birth something in us, we must be willing to be in it for the long haul. God does not want to entrust His purposes to those who love the excitement of starting something new but won't stick to it. If you do not nurture what God has birthed within you, it will die before accomplishing its God-ordained purpose.

At the same time that you embrace the responsibility of bringing forth what God gives you, you must also recognize that as something born of God matures, it may not look like you thought it would or act as you want it to. Eventually it will mature. But if you have done your parenting job well, God will be glorified in your offspring and they will go on to bear their own purposes for God.

My wife and I taught, disciplined, trained, mentored, and matured our children until they were properly prepared to fulfill the purpose for which they were born. Tim and Karen were the first to be married. Tim is the Chief Operating Administrator of Christian International Ministries Network and is fulfilling his apostolic-teacher calling. Sherilyn and Glenn are traveling full-time as prophets of God and serve with my other two children and 22 other couples as the CI Board of Governors. Tom and Jane are pastoring Christian International Family Church, which is located on the 72 acre CI Campus. The 60,000 sq. ft. building has an auditorium that seats over 1,200 people and is the place where we conduct our annual International Gathering of Apostles and Prophets conference. All three of our children and their spouses are in full-time ministry doing the work of the Lord. We still have contact with them and work with them, but we did our part in birthing, training, and preparing them to fulfill destiny.

Our children in turn are doing a good job of training up our eleven grandchildren in the things of God. Our grandchildren have all received prophecies that they have a calling and destiny to fulfill as members of the Body of Christ. Abraham's calling and destiny was restated through his son Isaac, his grandson Jacob, and his twelve great-grandchildren, the children of Israel. Our first great-grandchild arrived January 22, 2001. God is faithfully fulfilling His promises to me as a young man.

How Do You Parent Two Children While Pregnant with a Third Child?

In the last chapter I mentioned that we are currently raising a twelve year old Prophetic Movement, a two year old Apostolic Movement, and we are pregnant with the Saints Movement. In our family of ministry, we must help our older child grow on to adulthood, teach our younger child to walk (it will require much attention and nurturing for it to progress on to maturity), and carry our pregnancy to full-term.

Some well meaning friends in the ministry have tried to tell me that I am getting involved in too many ministry responsibilities. Like many pastors and leaders, I have the challenge of more invitations than time. Evelyn and I regularly ask our intercessors to pray that we will have God's wisdom in planning our schedule. But the things that God has birthed in my spirit and that we have raised up through the ministry of Christian International are our spiritual "children." CI has five major organizations that specialize in different ministries, all of which take different responsibilities in raising our children/ministries.

My wife gave birth to our son Tim in 1956, then Tom in 1959, and then suddenly 19 months later Sherilyn came along. Evelyn had the challenge of mothering two boys while being pregnant with a third child. If you have parented more than one child or were raised in a family of many children you know that it is more challenging to have more than one child. Mothers who have several children have to try to keep the teenagers and the junior-age children going while pregnant with another.

Can a married couple effectively parent more than one child? My wife's father was raised in a family of twelve children. Our worship leader, Dean Mitchum, was raised in a family of twelve children, of which he was the eleventh. He is a grown, married man with two natural children and two foster children and all of his 10 M's are in good order. His parents did a better job of raising him than I have seen some parents do who only raised one child. My good friend, Bishop Aaron Claxton, and his wife were each raised in a large family. One set of parents had 19 children and the other parents had 16 children. If God gives a big family then He gives grace to minister to each of the children and raise them to be adults. Only God knows how many children one set of parents can birth and raise responsibly.

Christian International and I have a responsibility for what God has birthed within us and through us. We must establish the truths of the Prophetic, Apostolic, and Saints Movements by preaching, teaching, and writing books and teaching manuals. We are training, activating, mentoring, and maturing those called to propagate these truths through our Ministry Training College, seminars, and conferences. Like growing children, they must be fed the milk of the Word until able to eat solid food, while continually being watered with Holy Spirit refreshing, enlightenment, and enablement. For proper development there must be sufficient exercise. This comes by activating those who have been taught, into a living experience, and then maturing to a proper balance in all these areas.

One of the secrets of successfully raising many children in one family is having the older children take areas of responsibility in housework and raising the younger children. No one can take the place of mom and dad, but the older children can become an extension of their parenting. While the older children are learning to be older brothers and sisters, they are helping raise the new generation of children, and learning skills of parenting they can use when they have their own children.

I have incorporated this principle in raising the big Christian International family. Those who were birthed into the apostolic-prophetic ministry through CI in the 1980's are now the senior leaders of the various ministries. This is true of the five presidents of our five major organizations and of four presidents of our international headquarters. The same is also true for the majority of our apostolic team couples who oversee CINC's 14 regional areas throughout the United States. They are functioning as grown children who are now parents with their own children. They are ministering to the new generation coming into apostolic-prophetic ministry. Many of those coming in now and growing up in the Apostolic/Prophetic Movement will become the grown married children who will parent the multimillions who will be coming into the family of God during the great harvest of souls which will take place during the Saints Movement.

` No Retiring

Just because my wife and I have successfully parented our children and they co-labor with us in the ministry doesn't mean we can retire and let them do the work. As I said at the outset, no one is too old to birth God's purposes. If you are still alive on planet earth, then the Lord has a purpose for you being here.

I'm going to keep building the kingdom as long as I can and if Jesus doesn't return before I go to be with Him, it's my desire to leave behind as much as possible for the work of the Lord. Like David left the blueprint and pattern for the building of the Temple, I want to leave prophetic revelation blueprints for God's patterned process for fulfilling His complete purpose on earth. As David gathered the resources for building the Temple, even so I want to leave millions of dollars of resources, land, equipment, and materials to be used for God's kingdom and tens of thousands of equipped saints to carry out the work and complete God's purpose for His Church.

Chapter 9

HOW TO ALIGN YOURSELF TO BIRTH GOD'S PURPOSE

"My little children, for whom I labor in birth again until Christ is formed in you." Gal. 4:19

What is Next on God's Agenda?

We have now entered into the third millennium of the Church. We who were ministers in the 1950's and taught the imminent return of Christ never believed that the mortal Church would still be here on earth in the year 2000. But here we are still a part of the mortal Church on earth.

Why hasn't the second coming of Jesus taken place yet? Some questions might lead us to some answers. Has the gospel of the kingdom of God been preached and demonstrated in every nation sufficiently to be a witness to the Lordship of Jesus Christ? Is the family of God complete? Does Jesus have all the members He needs to perfect the corporate Body of Christ? It requires a certain amount of cells for the human body to be perfectly functional. If every Church/Body of Christ member represented a cell, how many would it take to make a perfectly functional Body of Christ?   Does Christ have the quantity and quality of members He needs to have a perfected Church/Body, which He plans to use to fulfill His eternal work and purpose throughout the endless ages of eternity?   Has Christ's Church/Body come to the fulness of His life, way, and truth, or must there be more restoration of truth and more conformity to His image? (See Psalm 139:15-16; John 14:6; Acts 3:21; Romans 8:29; 1 Corinthians 12:27; 2 Corinthians 3:18; Ephesians 3:21, 4:11-15, 5:27; 1 John 3:2-3).

These questions can be answered by understanding a key divine Biblical principle.   If Christ Jesus has not come back to earth at what is called His "second coming," then that means there are more spiritual "comings" of Jesus in revivals for harvesting souls, restoring truth, and perfecting the saints.   If the literal coming has not taken place then there are more restoration movements to take place.[1]   According to Acts 3:21 there can be no final return of Christ until there is a final restoration:

> *Christ is held in heaven until the restoration of all things which have been spoken by the mouth of all God's holy prophets since the world began.*

This scripture refers to prophecies that must come to pass before Christ's second coming can take place, not His first coming.   In verse 18 Peter declared by the Holy Spirit that all the prophecies concerning Jesus' first coming as a suffering Savior, as the promised Messiah of Israel and Redeemer of all mankind, "He has thus fulfilled."

---

[1] See *The Eternal Church*, pp. 340-341.

Evangelical ministers and most Pentecostal ministers only see the prophecies concerning the world conditions that must come to pass, but see nothing needing to be fulfilled in and through the Church. However most Charismatic ministers and all apostolic-prophetic ministers see in the prophetic scriptures of the Old and New Testament many things yet to be fulfilled in and through the Church. God's family is not complete. More family members have yet to be born into God's family, more truth has yet to be restored, more equipping and perfecting of members of the Body of Christ in their membership ministries has yet to be done, and the corporate Church has to be brought to more unity and oneness with one another under the Head of the Church, Christ Jesus.

We have revealed where we have come from and where we are today, but where do we go from here? We know what we have done in the past, but what can we do today to be ready for tomorrow? When we receive the revelation that more things must be fulfilled we are motivated to seek the Lord for our part. So how does one do this?

Steps to Birth God's Purpose

The points we used earlier, illustrated by a man and woman becoming a married couple producing a family, reveal several things each person needs to do:

1. **You need to get a revelation and conviction concerning whether you and the present truth are meant for each other.** Are you compatible? Do your desires, vision, and theology line up with

what God is doing today? If not, are you willing to seek God for new vision? You must get a clear revelation of your membership ministry and destiny in Christ.

2. **Make a covenant like a marriage vow to God that you will stay with His purpose and ministry regardless of the ways it may affect your life.** In other words, you become a prisoner to the purpose of God. Remember, God will not let you conceive a revelation that is destined to bless His Church unless you are fully committed to bringing it forth and working with it until it reaches maturity.

3. **Maintain a close relationship with Jesus Christ until you get pregnant with present truth and the future purposes of God for yourself and His corporate Church.** Revelation is birthed from intimate relationship with God and His Word, prayer, and walking in His ways. When you are close enough to God to know His heart, the desires of your heart become aligned with His purposes.

4. **Maintain the pregnancy, by keeping faith and confidence in what you are pregnant with, until it progresses to God's time for its birth.** Do not abort the baby regardless of the persecution, rejection, difficulties, and inconveniences it may bring to your life. Keep interceding, warring, and standing in faith for the vision to become reality. Being pregnant with a spiritual restoration truth, a vision, a personal membership ministry, or a divine

purpose of God may continue for many years before God's time for birthing. Keep in mind that while a woman is pregnant others cannot see the baby inside, nor can she show it to anyone so that they can see what it looks like, but when it is born all can see the results of the waiting time. God will not leave us eternally pregnant. He will bring us to the time of birth (remember Isa. 66:9).

5. **Allow God to bring you into labor and birthing at His *kairos* time.** Be sensitive to His timing. Don't become impatient and try to force premature labor. Don't be discouraged if you have some false labor pains that don't produce. But press on until the Holy Spirit induces the true labor pains that produce the birth of the baby. Stay strong and courageous during the struggle of travail and birthing, knowing that the momentary affliction will produce a great result. Trust God to give you strength for fully birthing a healthy revelation or ministry that is destined to bless many.

6. **Grow the baby to maturity.** Make room in your life for a long-term commitment to the purpose of God. Be prepared to be a parent in the coming Saints Movement. Become equipped to teach, train, activate, mentor, and mature others in their ministry and in God's present truth and corporate purpose for His Church. Make sure you are fully

established in every restoration truth that has been restored to the Church over the last 500 years.[2]

If you are ready to commit to these things, you will find a prayer of commitment in the final chapter, along with a prophetic challenge and charge to all who desire to fully embrace God's purposes in their lifetime.

---

[2] To familiarize yourself with all restoration truth and Church ministry that has been restored, read pages 107, 189-209 in *Apostles, Prophets & the Coming Moves of God* and the Restoration of the Church Chart on page 52-53 in *Prophets and the Prophetic Movement.* For a more detailed study of the Protestant, Holiness, Pentecostal, and Charismatic restoration movements, read the section on Church restoration in the book, *The Eternal Church*, pages 114-306.

Chapter 10

CHALLENGE TO THREE PROPHETIC
AGE GROUPS

*"I write to you, little children, because you have known the Father.
I have written to you, fathers, because you have known Him who is
from the beginning. I have written to you, young men, because
you are strong, and the word of God abides in you, and you have
overcome the wicked one."* 1 John 2:13-14

I want to close by revealing some things that the Lord
shared with me in 1992. As I was talking to the Lord
about some particular things I said, "Lord, ever since my
early twenties I have preached about the Joshua generation. Expectations were that I would be part of that generation and cross over Jordan before I was thirty years old.
Now in a couple of years I will be twice that age." Jesus
began to share some encouraging and enlightening things
with me. He reassured me that I would be a part of the
Joshua generation, but that I was not of the new generation
group but of the older Joshua group.

To convey the reality of what God was seeking to
reveal, He used the three generations of myself, my
children, and my grandchildren. In 1992 our three
children were in their thirties and our grandchildren were

13 and under. He said, "Those 40 and older will be the generation that will cross over Jordan. Those your children's ages, 39 down to 14, will be the generation that will begin to dispossess the "-ites" of Canaan. And those 13 and under, including a generation yet to be born, will be the ones who will see the consummation of the ages, bring back the King, overcome all things, and see My kingdom established on planet earth."

At the present, in the year 2000, these age groups are eight years older. The first group would be those 48 and older, the second group those 22 to 47, and the last group those age 21 and younger, including those yet to be born. The group 48 and older will be the generals, lieutenants, and mature leaders who have been established in present truth. They will lead the Church into its end-time promised Canaan land. The participants age 22 to 47 will be the ones who drive out the "-ites" and possess Canaan by making sure the Apostolic and Prophetic Movements fulfill their destiny and purpose. They will become the prophetic-apostolic intercessors who will function like midwives, nurses, and doctors to help birth the Saints Movement. They will be the main propagators of the present restoration movements and the major leaders. Those age 21 and under will be the group that fulfills all things, overcomes the last enemy in Canaan, completes the way, and makes ready a people for the coming of the Lord. They are going to be the most radical, fanatical, unstoppable, unquenchable, dead-to-self, alive-to-God, possessing, overcoming, fearless, bold generation of God's people ever!

Take Action - Respond - Make A Prayer Commitment

It is no accident that you are reading these things now. You have a destiny to be part of one of these groups. Everyone has a strategic place destined for them in God's army.

Where you fit is not so much according to natural age as to the spiritual maturity that these age groups represent in the natural. In other words, a 60 year old who has just been born again and has become turned on to God's purposes would not necessarily be part of the older group. However, for the sake of simplicity, I will use the natural ages now to make the challenge to each group. These ages are as of the year 2000.

To Those Age 48 and Older

I challenge those 48 and older to have the Caleb spirit and attitude. Caleb declared to Joshua, when he requested the right to lead his tribe to take the land which he had claimed for himself when he originally spied out Canaan:

> *"Here I am this day, 85 years old. As yet I am as strong this day as on the day that Moses sent me; just as my strength was then, so now is my strength for war, both for going out and for coming in, therefore give me this mountain to go and take for my inheritance."* (Jos. 14:10-12)

I have been claiming this promise for years, that I will be as strong for warfare ministry at 85 as I was at 42. I have been, and will continue to be, a major leader in the apostolic and prophetic; however, I am not going to stop there. I am definitely pregnant with the Saints Movement.

I am moving the pregnancy along by preaching about it and writing a book on the revelation and scriptural reality of the coming Saints Movement.

Let us declare that we are not dead heads! We are not the over the hill gang. We are still warriors. We have the Caleb spirit and attitude! Although I am this age in the natural, yet my strength and vision is vibrant and alive. I can swing my sword and fight with the warriors. I will use my years of wisdom and maturity to help bring to maturity the twelve year old Prophetic Movement and the two year old Apostolic Movement and to carry and nurture the Saints Movement until it is birthed in the midst of the Church.

When I preached this message I asked all those 48 and older who were willing to be a Joshua and Caleb to stand and make this declaration. **If you are in this group and are ready to make a commitment to God,** lay your hand on this book to show your response, and declare this with us:

"I make a legal commitment in the spirit realm, like a legal marriage vow, to stay with God's purpose for me and the Saints Movement until birthed, then help bring it to maturity and fulfillment. I dedicate myself now to raise this child, to give all my resources to it, and to bring it forth to fulfill destiny. It is being recorded in heaven right now that I am making this covenant with God. I will be sold out for God's purposes. I will not abort. I will not stop. I will press on and possess my promised land. Amen."

To the Age Group 22 through 47

You are the group that must fully demonstrate the Apostolic/Prophetic Movement and bring forth the Saints Movement. You may not be the main demonstrators, but you will be the teachers, trainers, activators, and the ones who will go before and prepare the way. You have received a revelation that caused a conception within the womb of your spirit. There is something that has been activated in your spirit that will make you want to see God's last day apostles and prophets do the work of preparing the way and making ready a people for the coming of the Lord. Are you willing to stay in the womb until you are ready to be birthed? Now God is preparing you to be leaders, sergeants, lieutenants, and generals to help lead this great army, and to be demonstrators of His great power. Right now you are going to be the older brothers and sisters of the Saints Movement.

The next generation will work with all the babies that are going to be born into God's family. They are the main ones who are going to be the harvest reapers. But you are the major demonstrators and standard bearers, the ones who have to go out to prepare the way, demonstrate it, take the apostolic-prophetic on to fulfillment, and lay the foundation for the Saints Movement. There are some places where people don't even know there has been a Prophetic Movement. There are places that don't even know there are still apostles and prophets in the Church today. We have the divine commission to make this truth known throughout the Body of Christ around the world.

**If you are sincerely ready to commit to help
make this happen, pray this prayer of commitment:**

*"Father God, I am Your child. You birthed me with
a calling and destiny to birth something. There has been
a conception within the womb of my spirit. I have a vision
to see apostles and prophets fully restored. I have a desire
to be, to do, and to demonstrate the truth. Here I am, Lord.
I am committed. I make a vow, a marriage relationship
with You, that I will stay close to You until this is
accomplished. Now let the Saints Movement that I am
pregnant with begin to grow within me until miracles,
signs, wonders, and the supernatural are demonstrated
through my life. I will be an older brother/sister to the
Saints Movement. I will be whatever You want me to be,
and I will fulfill whatever part You assign to me. You are
writing my name in Your book of remembrance (Mal.
3:16). You wrote my name down today, afresh and anew.
God, I want You to be able to say, 'Child, I can depend on
you.' Here am I, Lord. Use me. Amen."*

To the 21 and Under Age Group

The teenagers, children, and babies being born are the ones
who are going to bring back the King. They must become
the most fanatical, radical, devil-hating, Jesus-loving,
fearless, bold, and courageous generation that has ever
lived. This is the generation that really excites my spirit,
for I know their destiny. I am believing God to keep me
alive and active another 20 to 30 years so that I can be with
this group in all that they are going to be and do.

If you are in this age group, you must come to the place where your life is the standard for showing those around you the way to live. You must come to the place where nobody can intimidate you about your Christianity or about your God. You must be convinced that Jesus Christ is the one and only true God. Jesus is the only Way, the only Truth, and the only Life. The world and old order Christians will call you fanatics, but you will not be a lukewarm generation, for you are going to get too fiery for the devil to handle. Become bold now! You do not have to wait until you are a certain age. Your generation is going to experience and demonstrate the supernatural kingdom of God until it is established and covers the earth as the waters cover the sea.

There is not just a youth revival coming but a youth revolution! You are going to the public schools, private schools, church schools, and home schools. A revolutionary revival is coming to schools from kindergarten through college. You will invade all areas of the world with the supernatural kingdom of God. Many will get activated by becoming involved in intercessory prayer walks, Bible studies, and spiritual renewal meetings. You are the **"Transition Generation."** Your group will be the generation that will fully manifest the Saints Movement, become the Army of the Lord, and bring forth the "Kingdom Establishing Movement" which will finalize the restoration of all things, releasing Jesus to come from heaven and take dominion over all the earth.

Jesus is still saying today that we should allow the children to come unto Him for He is going to use them mightily. Jesus is excited about this age group, for they will be the ones to bring Him back as King. Even now God is going to sovereignly visit the teenage and junior-age children, moving them into the Holy Spirit realm of visions and supernatural visitations. They will prophesy very specific things and heal the sick. They will receive such a revelation of Jesus that it will cause them to lose all fear of the devil and evil spirits. They will know that the smallest child of God, cleansed by the blood and clothed with the robe of righteousness and the garment of praise, can whip the biggest demon hell has to offer. They will be little David's, boldly going against and defeating great Goliath's.

This is not fanciful and wild imagination but reality. It has already been demonstrated during what was called the "Addulum Orphanage Revival" in China in 1952. Children in the orphanage got saved and filled with the Holy Spirit as a sovereign move of God swept into their midst. Those six to nine years old were used the most. They had numerous angelic visitations, visions of heaven and hell, and detailed dreams about people, places, and events. They were enabled to see into the spirit world of demons. It was so real that they chased the demons out of their midst and cast them out of people. The children would prophesy, quoting whole books of the Bible.

I challenge youth pastors to begin preaching and imparting this vision and faith to the youth. Believe for God's visitation and be prepared to allow it to happen when it starts.

Young people, get pregnant with this visitation. Get such a hunger and thirst until you are filled with God's righteousness, revolutionary revival, and another restoration move of God! Start preparing now so that you will be prepared to participate in all God is about to do. Your generation is going to experience all that the prophets have seen and longed to participate in. Do not miss your day of visitation, for you are a predestined and privileged generation.

The first step to take is to **let the Lord Jesus know that you are willing to fulfill His purpose for your age group.** If this is your strong desire, demonstrate your participation by laying your hand on this book and **pray this prayer of commitment:**

*"Father God, in Jesus Name, I present myself to You for Your purpose. I surrender my whole life--spirit, soul, and body--to You for Your use. I want to be one of those who are destined to be part of Your young Joshua group that will become the **Kingdom of God Demonstration and Transition Generation.** I do not understand all that this will mean in my head, but my heart says I receive and believe to become all that You want me to be. You are writing my name in Your record book now. I submit to Your process for spiritual conception, pregnancy, and birthing. Amen."*

An Apostolic Charge

When I preached this message and the groups finished praying these prayers, I made some apostolic decrees and prophetically prayed for them and their generation. By the power of the Holy Spirit, God can apply the same decrees and prophetic prayers to you who have prayed just now.

"Father God, in the name of Your Son Jesus Christ, I ask You to release upon those who have committed to You the five anointings You have given to me as Your Apostle-Prophet. May all who receive this message also receive the impartation of the:

1. *Apostolic/prophetic ministry*

2. *Family anointing*

3. *Reproducing and activating anointing*

4. *Team anointing for working together*

5. *Warrior anointing for warfare praise and prayer to possess and produce Your purpose.*

"Lord, let them receive a revelation conception and get pregnant with Your purpose for them, as individuals and as Your corporate Church. Give them the ability to conceive and bring forth Your destiny within the Church. If they are not already pregnant with the Saints Movement then we decree that the seed of the Saints Movement, and future movements such as the 'Army of the Lord' and the 'Kingdom Establishing Movement,' will be in all three of these age groups. May each one You have destined to become a fivefold minister fulfill this calling, especially apostles and prophets. Make them into apostolic and prophetic leaders in the local churches and in the marketplaces. Activate within them such revelation that they will become Your visionaries, miracle workers, and believers who cast out devils and heal the sick, demonstrating signs and wonders for Your glory. May they

please You in all they do, hastening the day of the return of Your dear Son, Christ Jesus. Amen."

I apostolically decree and prophetically charge you to know and fulfill your prophetic destiny! As you practice the principles of spiritual conception, pregnancy, and birthing you will bring forth God's purpose for your life and fulfill your destiny. We also agree and decree for you to come forth into God's destiny for His Church and planet earth, in Jesus' Name.

Come Forth Omega Generation!

*"Lord, we call forth those age 21 down to those yet to be born, for they are the **Transition Generation** to become the greatest ever **Demonstration Generation**. Lord, make them fanatics for You. They are destined to be the third and final group of the **Joshua Generation,** the **Omega Generation** of the mortal Church. Jesus, birth Your end-time purpose and zeal within them so that the zeal of the Lord of Hosts may perform this. (Isa. 9:7) Lord, I am pregnant with this last generation and I want to help birth every revelation they need to accomplish Your final work. We intercede now on behalf of this generation."*

This is the generation that Prophet David, the king, prophesied about in Psalm 102:12-22. These prophetic scriptures reveal who they are and what they shall accomplish. As verse 18 declares, *"This is written for the generation to come."*

It is the appointed time for you to come forth, *"Generation to Come."* You are the *Esther Generation* that has come to the kingdom for such a time as this. (Es. 4:14) The great cloud of witnesses in heaven is waiting for you to fulfill your ministry, for without you, they cannot be perfected. (Heb. 11:38-12:2) Not only are the heroes of the faith witnessing and waiting, but the whole creation is groaning in travail with laboring birth pangs and with earnest expectation for this *Transition Generation* to come forth and fulfill their destiny so that it can be "delivered from the bondage of corruption into the glorious liberty of the children of God." (Rom. 8:19-23) I implore all the age groups to do their part to bring the pregnancy to full-term that there may be a birthing. Older ones, you are the spiritual midwives to help bring forth the *Omega Generation.* As we read in Chapter Two, God has solemnly promised that He will deliver what has been shut up in the womb and definitely cause delivery to take place at the time of birth. (Isaiah 66:9) The woman is in labor pains to bring forth the man-child (the matured Church). He shall not be devoured by the dragon but shall take his throne rights alongside King Jesus and rule the nations with a rod of iron. (Rev. 12:5, 2:26-27)

Omega Generation, the Spirit and the Bride say, "Come!" The witnesses say, "Come!" The whole creation says, "Come!" It is the appointed time to birth and to come forth! It is all in, by, and through You, Lord Jesus. We pray for Your kingdom to come, and even more so, may You come, Lord Jesus!

Amen

BOOKS BY
DR. BILL AND EVELYN HAMON

BOOKS BY DR. BILL HAMON

Apostles,Prophets and the Coming Moves of God	13.99

Teaching manual or workbook not available yet.

Prophets and Personal Prophecy	13.99
Prophets and The Prophetic Movement	13.99
Prophets Pitfalls and Principles	13.99
The Eternal Church	13.99

Teaching manuals and workbooks are also available.

Prophetic Destiny and the Apostolic Reformation	6.95
Fulfilling Your Personal Prophecies	3.95

BOOKS BY EVELYN HAMON & OTHER AUTHORS

The Spiritual Seasons of Life (Evelyn Hamon)	3.95
God's Tests are Positive (Evelyn Hamon)	3.95
Dreams and Visions (Jane Hamon)	9.99
The Deborah Company (Jane Hamon)	9.99

AUDIO TEACHING TAPE SERIES

The Restoration & Destination-Church (Dr. Bill Hamon)	50.00
The Coming Saints Movement (Dr. Bill Hamon)	10.00
Principles to Live By (Dr. Bill Hamon)	30.00
Prophetic Pitfalls (Dr. Bill Hamon)	35.00
The 10 M's (Dr. Bill Hamon)	15.00
Plugging Into Your Spritual Gifts (Dr. Bill Hamon & Others)	30.00
Handling Life's Realities (Evelyn Hamon)	20.00
Dealing With Life's Challenges (Evelyn Hamon)	20.00

PROPHETIC PRAISE TAPES & CDS

Praise & Worship featuring Dean & Lisa Mitchum

People of a New Beginning; Here's My Heart; Show Your Power; Demonstration Generation; Holy Nation, Jump In The River

Praise & Worship featuring Robert Gay

Mighty Man of War; Roar, Lion of Judah; The God of Glory Thunders; Lord Sabaoth; The Shout of a King; Fan the Flame; Silencing the Enemy; Lord of the Breakthrough

Many more audio, video, cassettes, CDs and books available

To order these or other products by Dr. Bill & Evelyn Hamon call:

1-888-419-2432

or write:

CHRISTIAN INTERNATIONAL BOOKSTORE

5200 East Highway 98, Santa Rosa Beach, FL 32459

or order online:

www.cibookstore.com

Contact Christian International for exact shipping costs.
Prices subject to change without notice.

CHRISTIAN INTERNATIONAL MINISTRIES

Helping to restore prophets and apostles to the Body of Christ, so they can take their place alongside pastors, evangelists, and teachers to teach, train, and activate the saints into their ministries and see the Church fully matured for the Lord's return.

CHRISTIAN INTERNATIONAL NETWORK OF CHURCHES - CINC
Training, equipping, and accountability based on relationship for an international association of ministers and churches who have a heart to see God's apostles and prophets restored and the Body of Christ established in present truth.

CHRISTIAN INTERNATIONAL BUSINESS NETWORK - CIBN
Providing relationships and resources for the 98% of Christians whose primary calling is outside the local church. Gain clear vision, hear the voice of God for your business, and be equipped as a "minister in the market place" and public arena.

SCHOOL OF THEOLOGY - CIST
Quality biblical education through a systematic off-campus study program, from the fundamentals of the faith to present-truth prophetic and apostolic ministry. Courses of study available at all degree levels or for personal enrichment.

MINISTRY TRAINING COLLEGE - CI MTC
A residential college providing "hands on" ministry preparation for five-fold ministers and saints. Receive academic instruction, impartation through the Elijah/Elisha principle of mentoring, and experience in prophesying and ministering the gifts.

MANUAL FOR MINISTERING SPIRITUAL GIFTS - MSG
Over 30,000 saints have been trained to hear the voice of God and flow in the gifts of the Holy Spirit through this anointed tool. Sound biblical truth is followed by activation sessions. Certification to teach the manual available.

SEMINARS & CONFERENCES
We offer a variety of conferences, training seminars, and special events at our International Training Center in Santa Rosa Beach, Florida and at various locations in the U.S. and around the world. All conferences provide prophetic ministry to attendees.

RESOURCES
We offer books, teaching tapes, training manuals, videos, and praise & worship tapes and CD's focusing on the prophetic, apostolic, and present truth.

AND MUCH MORE!

CALL TODAY
850-231-2600
OR
VISIT OUR WEBSITE
WWW.CIMN.NET
TOLL-FREE SEMINAR LINE **1-800-388-5308**
P. O. BOX 9000, SANTA ROSA BEACH, FL 32459

International Training Centers

God is fulfilling the vision of Christian International to train and activate five-fold ministers and saints both nationally and internationally. CI has established headquarters on six continents: CI-Asia, CI-Australia, CI-Canada, CI-Europe, CI-India, and CI-South America, from which ministry and training for the nations have been launched.

CIMN International Headquaters

72 Acre Campus, Santa Rosa Beach, FL, USA

Dr. Bill Hamon

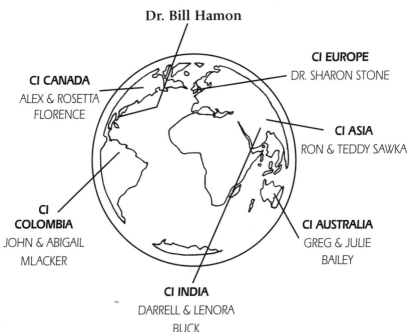

CI EUROPE
DR. SHARON STONE

CI CANADA
ALEX & ROSETTA FLORENCE

CI ASIA
RON & TEDDY SAWKA

CI COLOMBIA
JOHN & ABIGAIL MLACKER

CI AUSTRALIA
GREG & JULIE BAILEY

CI INDIA
DARRELL & LENORA BUCK

CHRISTIAN INTERNATIONAL BUSINESS NETWORK

Vision For Your Success

The vision of Christian International Business Network (CIBN) is to equip Christian business people to operate in the supernatural power of God and to practice biblical principles in the market place. In the day-to-day pressures of the business world, fortunes are made and lost based upon making the right decision at the right time. CIBN teaches, trains, activates and mentors Christian business leaders in how to apply biblical decision making principles in this complex and spirit-filled environment. CIBN also assists Christian business people in understanding their personal calling and identifying their talents and gifts. Further, CIBN operates as a resource and networking center, bringing together Christian business people of like-vision and purpose in order to see the Kingdom of God established in the earth today.

CIBN offers opportunities for training and assistance in business through its newsletter (Christian Business Today) training, seminars, local chapters and consulting services.

CALL TODAY
850-231-2600
OR
VISIT OUR WEBSITE
WWW.CIMN.NET
TOLL-FREE SEMINAR LINE **1-800-388-5308**
P. O. BOX 9000, SANTA ROSA BEACH, FL 32459

CHRISTIAN INTERNATIONAL MINISTRY TRAINING COLLEGE

A PROPHETIC / APOSTOLIC SCHOOL

ON-CAMPUS IN SANTA ROSA BEACH, FLORIDA

OUR VISION

Christian International MINISTRY TRAINING COLLEGE's vision is to teach and equip students in a practical and experiential way for prophetic / apostolic ministry. Our approach to teaching and learning is based on the Elijah - Elisha principle: the impartation of knowledge, experience and anointing through a mentor-student type relationship.

RECEIVE

One or two year on-campus ministry training.

An Associate Degree in Prophetic Ministry!

Powerful classroom teaching in vital areas like prophetic ministry, prayer, leadership, practical theology, pastoral counseling, worship etc...

Practical and supervised mentoring with major emphasis on personal prophetic ministry and a minor emphasis in counseling or arts & worship.

CINC
Christian International
Network of Churches

CINC is a Network of ministers and churches bonded together by a common heart and spirit. Our goal is to provide a place for both ministers and churches to be established in present-day truth and accountability.

CINC was raised up to minister to all five-fold ministers but especially to restore the offices of the apostle and the prophet as well as to maintain the truths, practices, and principles of the prophetic and apostolic movements in godly purity and Holy Ghost power. The mission of CINC is to develop a continuing network of local ministers and churches based upon committed relationships, submission to apostolic/prophetic oversight, mutual accountability, and faithful financial support.

A committed relationship suggests joining together in like-mindedness and submitting one to another in open, honest ways to accomplish mutual goals. Submission to apostolic/prophetic oversight requires that one be willing to permit the wisdom and counsel of the one in oversight to express itself in a loving, caring relationship. Becoming involved in such a relationship with CINC will offer new insight into the purpose and the need for accountability in the Church today.

NETWORK VISION

To bring about full restoration of the corporate Body of Christ by proclaiming present-truth for the purpose of establishing dynamic, growing local churches, building on the foundational ministries of the apostles and prophets.

CALL TODAY
850-231-2600
OR
VISIT OUR WEBSITE
WWW.CIMN.NET
P. O. BOX 9000, SANTA ROSA BEACH, FL 32459

Extension College

CI's Undergraduate and Graduate School of Theology was founded in 1967 to provide a quality academically sound biblical education through a systematic off-campus study program. CI was one of the first institutions of higher theological education to provide a program for those who could not afford to leave their work or ministry to pursue a traditional on-campus education. Now you can study at your own pace in the privacy of your home and earn a degree in theology.

CI provides a disciplined, organized and thorough curriculum of biblical studies in more than 300 semester hours of courses, ten major areas of study available from fundamentals of the faith to present truth prophetic ministry. Our educational philosophy can be best stated as *"education without indoctrination, doctrine without dogma."*

We believe **God has established the local church to train,** disciple, raise up and send out ministries to change the world for Christ. The *Christian International Extension College program* was developed in 1970 to provide the local church with the tools to establish an "in-house" Bible college for training their own saints and ministers. CI's Extension College Program provides resource materials, curriculum and over 30 years of expertise to assist local churches in developing their own Bible training center.

CALL TODAY
850-231-2600
OR
VISIT OUR WEBSITE
WWW.CIMN.NET
P. O. BOX 9000, SANTA ROSA BEACH, FL 32459

"The Eternal Church" is an exciting panoramic view of the Bride of Christ in Her birth, growth, maturity, marriage and eternal ministry of reigning with Christ Jesus from New Earth over God's endless domain. 395 pages $13.99

Books by:
Dr Bill Hamon

"Apostles, Prophets and the Coming Moves of God" will enlighten and enable all who are called and chosen to co-labor with Christ to fulfill the coming moves of God. It is for all those who are committed to making ready a people, preparing the way by restoring all things. This will enable Christ Jesus to be released from heaven to return for His Church and establish His kingdom over all the earth. 299 pages $13.99

Books by: Dr Bill Hamon

"Prophets and Personal Prophecy" It is the biblical manual on prophets and prophetic ministry. Many scriptural proofs plus exciting biblical and life experiences revealing the proper guidelines for receiving, understanding and fulfilling God's personal words to individuals, churches and nations. More than 150,000 in print in eight different languages. 218 pages. **$13.99**

"Prophets and the Prophetic Movement" A complete overview of the Prophetic Movement, its purpose and place in Church history in fulfilling God's ultimate destiny for His Church. Only in this book do you find the all important Seven Principles for determining a true restorational move of God.

Standards are given for discerning the differences between supernatural manifestations of Church prophets and people involved in the New Age, occult and other groups which manifest the supernatural. 227 pages **$13.99**

"Prophets Pitfalls and Principles" It reveals the pitfalls of weed seed attitudes, character flaws, and prophet syndromes found in the lives of several biblical prophets. The 10 M's for maintaining and maturing one's life and ministry are listed and explained. Answers are given to nineteen of the most common and complicated questions asked about prophets and personal prophecy. 224 pages. **$13.99**

Fulfilling Your Personal Prophecy

By:

Dr Bill Hamon

Pastors, make sure all of your leadership and members have their own copy of this vital booklet. **Everyone who thinks they have received a personal word from God needs this booklet.** Buy in quantity and give one to each person who receives a Personal Prophecy through your ministry.

PROPHETIC DESTINY & THE APOSTOLIC REFORMATION

By:

Dr Bill Hamon

"*Prohpetic Destiny and the Apostolic Reformation*"

This Book has a Threefold Purpose:

(1).Our first objective is to reveal to all saints what the Holy Spirit is seeking to accomplish in this day and hour. Everyone needs to know what is happening in the Church today and how it is working together to fulfill God's ultimate purpose.

(2).We want everyone to know that we are in the midst of a major restoration movement. The Prophetic-Apostolic Movements are destined to bring full restoration of the Prophet and Apostle ministries into the Church.

(3).Along with the importance of the others is the great need for all those who are called of God to understand the Process He takes us through to fulfill our prophetic destiny. Since the Prophetic Movement has produced a great company of prophets, thousands of Christians are receiving personal prophecies confirming and revealing fivefold callings and membership ministries in Christ's Church.

I pray that this book will be a blessing to all who read it. May we all have ears to hear what the Holy Spirit wants to say to us from what I have written in these pages.

EVELYN HAMON'S
BOOKS AND TAPE SETS

"God's Tests are Positive"

Evelyn reveals life giving truths essential to being a victorious overcomer. Discover how God's tests are His proving grounds for promoting, perfecting and prospering us. Biblical stories and personal life experiences are shared with the reader. If you have gone through some trials and tests that didn't seem to be positive to you this book will reveal truth that will set you free. You will be able to live with greater peace and joy after reading this book..

$3.95

"*The Spiritual Seasons of Life*" In this book, **Evelyn** gives a practical, natural look at the spiritual storms of our lives. She brings an uplifting and encouraging message that will help you to succeed in weathering life's changes.

$3.95

In this tape series, **Evelyn** offers encouragement and practical application for growing through the stages of God, determination in destiny, family life in ministry, and husband & wife relationships. **$20.00** (Four 90 minute tapes)

In this tape series, **Evelyn** shares wisdom and insight on the principles of progress & promotion, divine flexibility, spiritual seasons, and maintaining a positive attitude. **$20.00** (Four 60 minute tapes)

Teaching Manuals for
Prophets & Personal Prophecy,
Prophets & the Prophetic Movement,
Prophets Pitfalls & Principles.
The Eternal Church

Easy to use design follows books clearly

Contains additional information, scriptures and illustrations

Divided into sections for teaching in just weeks

Has an in-depth study guide for each chapter of the book

Each section has a handy teaching outline for pulpit use

Attractive type styles for a professional, clean look

High quality 3-ring binder with insert for cover and spine

Layout and approach makes it comfortable for those just becoming familiar with the prophetic

In-depth study makes it valuable to the most experienced minister

Satisfaction guaranteed or a full refund!

Workbooks for
Prophets & Personal Prophecy,
Prophets & the Prophetic Movement,
Prophets Pitfalls & Principles.
The Eternal Church

Indispensable for fully understanding the truths presented in the *Prophets and Personal Prophecy* book, *Prophets and the Prophetic Movement* book, *Prophets Pitfalls and Principles* book, *The Eternal Church* book. The workbooks uses a series of questions from each chapter of the books, followed by research assignments that delve into the complex and fascinating realms of the prophetic.

EARN COLLEGE CREDIT

College credit can be earned by completing the workbook (you can take it now and enroll later.) Request a CI College inquiry packet for more information.

The Coming Saints' Movement

• • • •

What's next for the Church? Essential insights concerning the next restorational move of God. A must for those who want to be a part of God's last moves. Revelation of God's purpose for the Saints' Movement and what it will accomplish in the Church and the world. **$10.00** (Two 90 minute tapes)

Principles to Live By

• • • •

Bishop Bill Hamon presents six major Biblical principles that have helped him fulfill 50 years of successful Christian living and 47 years of ministry. **$30.00** (Six 90 minute tapes)

Plugging Into Your Spiritual Gifts

• • • • • •

CI's finest ministers in an array of teaching on the gifts of the Holy Spirit. This tape series will bring encouragement and build up your faith to manifest the gifts God has placed within you. **$30.00** (Six 60 minute tapes)

Dr. Bill Hamon's Tape Sets

The 10 M's

This powerful series was developed to help you mature in and maintain your ministry. This series investigates 10 major areas of our personal lives which we need to continually examine and correct if we are to prove ourselves to be true ministers of God. **$15.00** (Three 60 minute tapes)

Prophetic Pitfalls

This exciting tape series is an in-depth look at the pitfalls that face today's Christians. Dr. Hamon uses biblical characters to disclose the subtle satanic pitfalls which can cause leadership and saints to fall. **$35.00** (Seven 60 minute tapes)

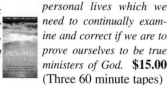

Another dynamic

 *Tape Set of*

Dr. Bill Hamon's

The Restoration and the Destination of the Church

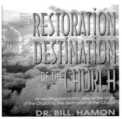

A heavenly satellite overall view of the Church from its origination to its ultimate destination. The greatest information available on the progressive restoration of the Church unto its end time ministry and eternal destiny. The history and future of the Church from a Prophets view.

$50.00 (Ten 90 minute tapes)

INTRODUCING

MANUAL
for
Ministering Spiritual Gifts
&
Student Workbook

"The Manual For Ministering Spiritual Gifts advances saints out of the realm of theory and brings them into a living experiential reality of God's graces. It is a manual designed for doing the Word, not just hearing it. This Manual helps teach, train, mature and develop saints in the gifts of the Spirit while helping leadership to prepare qualified saints for use in various facets of team ministry."

Dr. Bill Hamon

President & Founder of CI

Pastor, this manual will benefit your church and you...

It will activate the gifts and ministries of the saints by providing 13 weekly sessions along with 16 corresponding spiritual exercises.

It will stir and motivate your people towards spiritual ministry and their individual stewardship responsibilities of God's graces.

It will develop and mature your people in spiritual ministry without producing "spiritual spooks."

It will deepen and strengthen your people's relationship with God as they are taught and challenged to hear His voice.

It will furnish opportunity for church members to receive college credit for spiritual training through CI's School of Theology

The Manual for Ministering Spiritual Gifts is available to those pastors who have become certified trainers. For information concerning certification for use of the Manual for Ministering Spiritual Gifts please call or write to:

CHRISTIAN INTERNATIONAL MINISTRIES NETWORK

PO Box 9000, Santa Rosa Beach, FL 32459-9000

(850)231-2600 ext. 650

"***Dreams and Visions***" What is God saying in your dreams? How do you know if a dream is from God? What should you do when a dream contains a warning? Jane Hamon cuts through psychological jargon and cultural mumbo-jumbo to give you a clear, biblical understanding of the language of dreams-and how to discern the voice of the Lord as He communicates His purpose for your life. 172 pages $9.99

"***The Deborah Company***" God is releasing keys of revelation and spiritual principles that will unlock the latent potential of power in the Church and bring strategic breakthrough in these important days. Women will have a unique part to play in this last day army that God is assembling. The time is at hand in which God is activating the gifts which have been deposited by His Spirit into every blood-bought, Spirit-filled believer, regardless of gender. It is a day for women to step out from under their cloaks of inactivity and step into their God-ordained identities as active, vibrant members of the Body of Christ. 117 pages $9.99